On BLOODSTAINED FIELD II

132 More Human Interest Stories
of the Campaign
and Battle of Gettysburg

By
Gregory A. Coco

DEDICATION

This book is dedicated to the *Gettysburg Battlefield Preservation Association* for its important work in attempting to preserve battlefield land not under the protection of the National Park Service. Please send your contributions to this worthy organization at P.O. Box 1863, Gettysburg, PA 17325.

ACKNOWLEDGEMENTS

My sincere thanks go out to the kind and generous people who assisted me in various ways during this project. First and foremost to Cindy L. Small for the many hours she has spent typing, editing and encouraging this second volume. Also to Kathleen Georg Harrison, Robert H. Prosperi, John S. Heiser, Edmund J. Raus, Jr., Daniel E. Fuhrman, Edward F. Guy and Dean S. Thomas, for their many contributions. I am, as always, in your debt, and you all are most certainly friends beyond compare.

CONTENTS

FOREWORD

We know much about the Battle of Gettysburg: The great captains wrote their official reports and, in turn, have been glorified by their biographers. Military historians have studied the tactics and evolutions of battle, analyzed the terrain, and have packaged their findings in formal studies. Statisticians have counted and re-counted the numbers engaged and the casualties and have even told us which weapons inflicted the most wounds. But so often the stories of the common soldiers, just like the soldiers themselves, have gone un-noticed. Fortunately history is much more than just facts and dates, and in "On The Bloodstained Field II" editor Gregory Coco brings together a collection of 132 stories as recalled by the soldiers who fought here.

Greg Coco has spent years studying the Battle of Gettysburg and these stories have been gleaned from the volumes of books and articles written since the last shot was fired. As a combat veteran himself, Coco realizes that a soldier leaves the battlefield with many memories, but rarely an understanding of the grand scheme of battle. These recollections are brief, some of them only a few lines long, but they are the memories that the men took home. The horrors of battle are tempered by a soldier's good humor and the grand strategies are much less important than finding the next meal. We will never have the opportunity to talk with the men who fought at Gettysburg, but "On the Bloodstained Field" gives them one more chance to tell their story.

Robert H. Prosperi
Gettysburg, Pennsylvania
March 1989

INTRODUCTION

"It seemed to me as if every square yard of ground, for many square miles, must have its blood stain."

—Lt. George G. Benedict
12th Vermont Infantry

In early July of 1987 I had the opportunity to publish a small booklet entitled *On The Bloodstained Field,* which comprised a collection of 130 human interest stories pertaining to the Campaign and Battle of Gettysburg. The book was well received, enabling me to have initiated a second printing soon afterwards, and now a third which will be ready for distribution before the summer of 1989.

All of which brings me to the little volume you are now holding. This text, *On The Bloodstained Field II,* is an attempt to follow my previous publication with a second edition of all *new* material; 132 additional human interest stories, entirely pertinent to the terrible but fascinating Battle of Gettysburg.

The reader should find no repetition here even if he or she has read part one. Each individual account presented is an original, gleaned from hundreds of sources, such as letters, diaries, memoirs, regimental histories, and newspapers. All will shed new light on the battle since they were inspired by the men, women, children, soldiers and civilians who participated in the actual events that we now, over a hundred years later, can only imagine.

It is my belief that history should never be written solely by historians using "official sources," for often the final product has discarded the important human element. The following stories will then, generally portray people in situations where events have made it almost impossible for them to control their destinies.

In closing this introduction, I thank you for your interest in this important chapter of our history and sincerely hope you find much enjoyment and reflection within these pages. The final paragraph was composed by a veteran of the Civil War who served with the 140th Pennsylvania Infantry at Gettysburg. Although written more than seventy years ago it is still eloquent and significant today:

> Thank God, the time has come, for which so many brave men longed and prayed, in those dark and evil days, when all these scenes of strife are only memories. But, may God forbid that the time should ever come when the evidences which yet remain should fail to recall in the generations following the reality and magnitude of the struggle and the costliness of the sacrifice by which the blessings of permanent peace, Union and Liberty have been secured.

Gregory A. Coco
February 10, 1989

LIST OF STORIES

PART I

The Campaign: June 15 – June 30, 1863

Simon the Mule

While on the march into Pennsylvania in late June, 1863, during what was to become known as the Gettysburg Campaign, Captain F. M. Colston, serving with Alexander's Confederate Artillery Battalion of Longstreet's Corps, remembered the following incident concerning a friend in the cavalry.

Jim had lost his horse, and possessed himself of a white mule named Simon. He became very proud of his mule, and was loud in his praises. 'He never gets tired, lives on nothin' and has got more sense than the general,' asserted Jim. But one day a squad was enjoying a dinner with a sympathetic farmer when a sudden alarm was given. 'Run, boys, run; the Yankees are coming.' There was mounting in hot haste, and some escaped by the front gate and some by the rear. Jim dashed at the front gate; but Simon, displaying his mule nature for the first time, balked. Jim wheeled him around and drove at the rear gate, but Simon balked again. Poor Jim looked over his shoulder, saw the bluecoats rapidly approaching, threw his arms around Simon's neck, and called in agonizing tones: 'O Simon, for God's sake, go somewhere!'

Mud March

Captain Colston also observed this humorous episode along the route into Pennsylvania.

"On this march the dirt road was churned into a mud about the consistency of molasses and about six inches deep. As one of the Texas regiments was marching along in it one of the 'boys' with a ragged hat on and a general don't-care look, called out to a comrade, using strong adjectives: 'Damn it, Bill, put your foot down flat and don't kick up such a dust.' "

All "Railed" Up

On a muddy and miserable day during the Gettysburg Campaign an amusing incident took place; here described by Confederate D. A. Dickert, one of Kershaw's command. It is amusing, of course, to the reader, but may not have been to some of the participants.

Orders had been given when on the eve of our entrance into Maryland, that 'no private property of whatever description should be molested.' As the fields in places were enclosed by rail fences, it was strictly against orders to disturb any of the fences. This order had been religiously obeyed all the while, until (a) night [June 13] on the top of the Blue Ridge.

A shambling, tumble-down rail fence was near the camp of the Third South Carolina, not around any field, however, but apparently to prevent stock from passing on the western side of the mountain. At night while the troops lay in the open air, without any protection whatever, only what the scrawny trees afforded, a light rain came up. Some of the men ran to get a few rails to make a hurried bivouac, while others who had gotten somewhat damp by the rain took a few to build a fire.

As the regiment was formed in line next morning, ready for the march, Adjutant [Y. J.] Pope came around for company commanders to report to Colonel [James D.] Nance's headquarters. Thinking this was only to receive some instructions as to the line of march, nothing was thought of it until met by those cold, penetrating, steel-gray eyes of Colonel Nance. Then all began to wonder 'what was up.' He commenced to ask, after repeating the instructions as to private property, whose men had taken the rails. He commenced with Captain [R. E.] Richardson, of Company A.

'Did your men take any rails?'
'Yes, sir.'
'Did you have them put back?'
'Yes, sir.'
'Captain Gary, did your men use any rails?'
'Yes, sir.'

16

'Did you have them replaced?'

'No, sir.'

And so on down to Company K. All admitted that their men had taken rails and had not put them back, except Captain Richardson. Then such a lecture as those nine company commanders received was seldom heard. To have heard Colonel Nance dilate upon the enormity of the crime of 'disobedience to orders,' was enough to make one think he had 'deserted his colors in the face of the enemy,' or lost a battle through his cowardice. 'Now, gentlemen, let this never occur again. For the present you will deliver your swords to Adjutant Pope, turn your companies over to your next officer in command, and march in rear of the regiment until further orders.'

Had a thunder bolt fallen, or a three hundred-pound Columbiad exploded in our midst, no greater consternation would they have caused. Captain Richardson was exonerated, but the other nine Captains had to march in rear of the regiment during the day, subject to the jeers and ridicule of all the troops that passed, as well as the negro cooks.

'Great Scott, what a company of officers!' 'Where are your men?' 'Has there been a stampede?' 'Got furloughs?' 'Lost your swords in a fight?' were some of the pleasantries we were forced to hear and endure. Captain [John K.] Nance, of Company G, had a negro cook, who undertook the command of the officers and as the word from the front would come down the line to 'halt' or 'forward' or 'rest,' he would very gravely repeat it, much to the merriment of the troops next in front and those in our rear.

Near night, however, we got into a brush with the enemy, who were forcing their way down along the eastern side of the mountain, and Adjutant Pope came with our swords and orders to relieve us from arrest. Lieutenant Dan Maffett had not taken the matter in such good humor, and on taking command of his company, gave this laconic order, 'Ya hoo!' (That was the name given to Company C.) 'If you ever touch another rail during the whole continuance of the war, G-d d--n you, I'll have you shot at the stake.'

'How are we to get over a fence,' inquired someone.

'Jump it, creep it, or go around it, but death is your portion if you ever touch a rail again.'

Tradeoff

Charlie McCurdy, a schoolboy living in Gettysburg, related a story which shows that the thrifty Pennsylvania German or "Dutchman" could meet his equal in the clever ways shown by this particular Scotch-Irish

17

farmer.

My uncle, who lived on a fine estate near the mountains on the line of the Confederate advance, told me of a little incident that gave a homely, human touch to the war. During the march towards Gettysburg two Confederate soldiers came up the little lane that led to his residence and told him they needed a wagon as theirs had broken down and would have to take one of his. He asked them what had happened to it and they said one of the wheels had collapsed. He said that, as they needed only a wheel, there was no occasion to take a whole wagon and suggested that if one could be found to fit it would fill their needs. They agreed to this and went off with a wheel.

Maybe they were farmers and forgot for a moment that they were dealing with an enemy.

Footsore

At the 1889 dedication of the monument to the 139th Pennsylvania Infantry at Gettysburg, Captain William P. Herbert told his audience this story of an incident on the forced march into Pennsylvania which occurred about the middle of June, 1863.

I see the faces of Company I's boys before me, who, after their shoes were worn out, tied up their feet in cloths to protect them from the hot sand, and tramped cheerfully on. Some of you will remember big Joe Walker, of Company C. Corporal Walker had been most liberally endowed by nature in a physical way, and had equally large 'understandings.' Joe and his chum, Sam Grinder, had made requisition upon the quartermaster, each for a pair of number 'twelves;' but as every case of shoes did not have usually more than one of that size, the quartermaster was not able to honor their order just at that time. Joe's shoes had given out. One day he was stepping out in as soldierly a way as possible with bare feet. He was on a little path by the roadside. One of his comrades called out, 'Hello, Joe, how are you getting along with those feet? That is pretty hard luck.' The old veteran replied promptly: 'Oh, I am all right. If the Johnny rebs are going up to Pennsylvania, they will find me there too, if I have to wear these feet up to the stumps.' Joe got there, and did his duty too.

Some time afterwards, Walker was wounded and lost one of his legs by amputation in another campaign in Virginia.

Another Knapsack

In the first volume of *On The Bloodstained Field,* there is a story about a woman in Chambersburg who found the knapsack of her dead husband in the ranks of a passing Alabama regiment.

Since that time, I have located yet another story which is similar. The chances of one of these events taking place are very rare. However, to find two, is a startling coincidence.

W. A. Nabours, 5th Texas Infantry, reported this strange and very sad scene:

> We marched across the Blue Ridge Mountains into the Shenandoah Valley and to the Potomac, crossing into Maryland early in the morning. We marched entirely across the State in one day and camped in Pennsylvania that night. . . . As our soldiers were marching along the road near this camp an old lady hailed one and asked him where he got his knapsack. The soldier told her that he took it from a dead Yankee at Chancellorsville. On the side of the knapsack was the name of its former owner, regiment, and company in large letters. The old lady replied: 'That was my son.' The soldier stopped at once, took his own things out, and gave it to the lady, who seemed to appreciate it very much.

These captured knapsacks must have been fairly common. James A. L. Fremantle, a visiting Englishman with Robert E. Lee's Army of Northern Virginia during the campaign, reported:

"The knapsacks of the [Confederates] still bear the names of the Massachusetts, Vermont, New Jersey, or other regiments to which they originally belonged."

So, evidently, the old story of how the Rebels marched unencumbered with knapsacks is not totally true. It appears that in some cases just a simple blanket rolled and slung across the shoulder was not enough baggage for some Southerners after all.

Captured Civilians

A fact not generally known is that during the Gettysburg Campaign the invading Confederates took several Pennsylvania civilians into their ranks as punishment or to generate fear, and actually "kidnapped" a few men for various reasons, taking them back to military prisons in Virginia upon the Southern army's return. Here are a few examples:

A Mrs. Keefauver lived with her husband on a farm several miles out of town on the Emmitsburg Road. She remembered that when the Confederates first visited the area prior to the battle, her husband, in an attempt to save his property, told the Rebels that he was sympathetic to their cause. Mrs. Keefauver said that soon after this remark a general officer, taking the farmer at his word, promptly equipped him with a cartridge box and rifle and forced him into the Confederate ranks.

Curiously, this same type of incident occurred again, but this time within the Union Army. On or about July 1, while marching from Emmitsburg, Maryland, the 7th New York Infantry, commanded by Colonel M. W. Burnes, met an irate farmer who demanded twenty-five cents for payment due when the soldiers took a portion of his fence down. Colonel Burnes promptly "ordered him into the ranks and marched him six miles."

One of the best accounts of this kind is told in the biography of Emanuel G. Trostle who lived along the Emmitsburg Road, just south of Gettysburg. Prior to the battle he was visited by a Confederate colonel who ordered him (and his wife, Mary Plank, and their child), to quickly leave the farm as their lives were in danger. (Mr. Trostle was crippled at the time and walked with the aid of a staff and crutch.) The family was escorted through the pickets, but upon returning the next day, Trostle was for some unknown reason taken captive.

Completing this story, an Adams County historian said:

> He was taken to the battlefield [some time later], expecting to be paroled, but the firing opened before the parole could be made out. He was taken to Staunton, Virginia, walking the entire distance of 175 miles; was on the road six days, and for three days had not a mouthful to eat. He was detained in Richmond prisons, Libby, Castle Thunder, Hell's Delight, and Salisbury, North Carolina; in all of twenty-two months. It was reported that he had been killed. . . . After his release, he returned home feeling better than he had ever felt before.

A visitor to the battlefield on July 7, John B. Linn verified the fact that Trostle was indeed captured by the Rebels. After speaking on the subject to Mrs. Joseph Sherfy who also lived on the Emmitsburg Road, he wrote in his diary: "Mrs. S. told us the rebels had taken with them one of the Pitzers, one named Trostle and one named Patterson."

In Cold Blood

After General George H. Steuart's brigade of General Johnson's Confederate division entered McConnellsburg, Pennsylvania, on June 24, 1863, they remained two days. As one of the units in Lee's advance, they carefully combed the area gathering horses and cattle and other supplies to be used by the Rebel main force as it entered Pennsylvania. On June 26, Steuart's brigade moved on to Fort Loudon, where it remained for a short time, rounding up additional stock. After the brigade left this small village, two Rebel soldiers (probably stragglers hunting for more loot), were inadvertently left behind. These unfortunate men were rounded up near the center of town by several citizens who were recently discharged Union soldiers. A short time later they were murdered in cold blood. The Confederates were unarmed and had surrendered, but they were simply led away and shot. Afterwards, the two Southerners were buried in the town cemetery.

Even as late as 1970 these men were still suffering further inequity by having United States flags placed on their graves each Memorial Day. The flag obviously represented a country they did not die for.

Of the civilians who shot these harmless soldiers, it can readily be understood why Jonathan Swift called *mankind* "the most pernicious race of little odious vermin that nature ever suffered to crawl upon the surface of the earth."

The Fight at the Witmer Farm

Several days prior to the actual Battle of Gettysburg, a small military action occurred just north of the town. This incident made no difference one way or the other in the final outcome of the campaign. However, it is interesting in itself, and worth enumerating here.

On Friday, June 26, the 26th Pennsylvania Emergency Militia Regiment, under Colonel William Jennings, arrived in Gettysburg under orders from General D. N. Couch to delay the Confederate advance if possible. This unit of about 750 men was very inexperienced – one company had just recently been students at Pennsylvania College in Gettysburg. Few, if any, of these troops had any previous military training whatsoever.

Near midmorning on that Friday, the regiment accompanied by Captain Robert Bell's cavalry company, took position on the Chambersburg Pike near the banks of Marsh Creek. The Confederates were soon discovered moving toward Colonel Jenning's bivouac. Assuming that his small force could not hinder the Rebels, he quickly formed ranks. Swinging into a column of march, his militia began moving away to the northeast along a dirt road which soon intersected the Mummasburg-Hunterstown Road, a mile-and-a-half east of Mummasburg. This march took the 26th Emergency to safety away from the Southern force which continued moving along the pike toward Gettysburg.

About midafternoon, still unseen by any Confederates, Colonel Jenning's exhausted and straggling regiment reached Bayly's Hill (four-and-one-half miles due north of Gettysburg). The tired soldiers rested on the east side of the hill at the farm of Catherine and Henry Witmer. Built in 1860, Witmer's brick farmhouse stood nearby. The house's front yard along the road boasted a well which soon cooled the parched throats of the thirsty militia. While the soldiers paused here, Witmer's family of eight children began to bake bread and otherwise assist the men.

Meanwhile, the 17th Virginia Cavalry under Colonel William French, followed by two brigades of infantry, had taken up the chase of the militia. Suddenly coming over Bayly's Hill to the west, French's cavalry surprised the resting Pennsylvanians. Everything became confusion and chaos while Jennings attempted to form his men behind a rail fence which stood along a sunken lane opposite the Witmer farmhouse. Shots were fired by both sides; a few Confederate saddles were emptied, and a militia man named Bailey was hit in the head by a bullet. Finding it impossible to form a proper defensive line, Colonel Jennings led his men eastward across a small brook and then to high ground near the Good Intent Schoolhouse. Here they waited for a renewed attack by French who, in the meantime, decided to call off any further hostilities. The Confederates gathered about 170 Union men as prisoners but they were later paroled. Jennings' 26th Regiment then began a dreary rain-soaked march northward, finally arriving back in Harrisburg at 2 p.m. on Sunday, June 28.

Today, the scene of this exciting and unexpected attack is almost unchanged from its 1863 appearance. The present day visitor can stop near Witmer's old brick house and pause for a while at the well and the sunken road, contemplating the plight of a group of panicked boys who forever left their imprint on the site so many years ago.

NOTE: Unfortunately, as of this writing, Bayly's Hill is now advertised for sale and will probably be developed in the very near future.

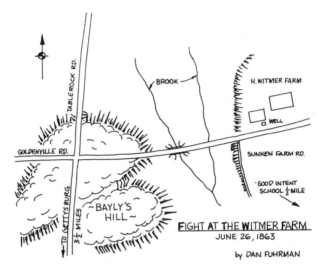

FIGHT AT THE WITMER FARM
JUNE 26, 1863

by DAN FUHRMAN

Henry Witmer farmhouse with Bayly's Hill in the left background.

A Mysterious Visitor

Sunday, June 28, 1863, found lead elements of Lee's Confederate Army under General John B. Gordon, drawn up near Wrightsville, a small village on the east bank of the Susquehanna River. The town was defended by a Northern militia force commanded by Colonel Jacob Frick. During that day a short bombardment of the town and its defenses convinced Frick that his small command would be no match for Gordon's veteran troops. The village was abandoned and as soon as his men were safely over the river in Columbia, he destroyed the 5,620-foot, covered bridge. The Confederates entered Wrightsville and helped to extinguish the burning bridge that threatened the whole community. Gordon's men remained overnight, many billeting themselves in houses vacated by the citizens.

One of the homes so used was owned by the Samuel Smith family and was located on Locust Street across from the Methodist Church. The Smiths had a son named Silas who had joined the Union army earlier in the war. When he went off to fight, the family had given him a pocket testament inscribed with his name and home address on the flyleaf. Silas never returned to that home. He had been wounded, taken prisoner by the Rebels, and had died in a Southern hospital.

After the invaders had gone, the Smiths returned to their home to find Silas' testament on a table in one of the rooms which had been used by the Confederates. No message was left and nothing had been stolen or disturbed anywhere in the house.

Who left the boy's bible was never determined.

A Terrible Mistake

During the Confederate invasion this unusual and tragic incident occurred in Codorus Township near Hanover, Pennsylvania.

About midmorning on June 29, General George G. Meade, commanding the Union army which was now in the vicinity of Frederick, Maryland, wrote an important dispatch concerning the army's movements toward Pennsylvania. A courier was entrusted with the dispatch with orders to transmit it to General Henry W. Halleck in Washington. Telegraph lines had been cut in western Maryland, causing the courier to reroute to the lower end of York County. At 9 p.m., he reached the village of Marburg, four-and-a-half miles southeast of Hanover, where he halted for something to eat.

After his supper, the lone courier rode toward Glen Rock where a line to Baltimore and Washington was reported to be in operation. He apparently lost his way, and as he approached Green Ridge he stopped at the farmhouse of George Bair and called out for help in finding the correct route. It was midnight, and the frightened farmer, who spoke no English, thought the soldier at the door was a Rebel – one of the enemy now on Pennsylvania soil. A shot rang out from the house, and the courier fell dead from his horse.

In great distress after the shooting, Bair surrendered himself to military authorities in Frederick where he was later tried and acquitted by a military court.

The soldier, a New York cavalryman, was buried at "Stone Church" near where he was killed. His remains were subsequently claimed and removed by his father several months later. The dispatches were found at the time of the incident and were sent to the War Department. They can be read in the *Official Records of the War of the Rebellion,* Volume XXVII, Part 1, page 66.

Tanned

On June 30, 1863, a cavalry skirmish took place about fifteen miles east of Gettysburg in Hanover, Pennsylvania, between forces commanded by J. E. B. Stuart and Judson Kilpatrick. In this fight, Abraham Folger, Company H, 5th New York Cavalry, captured an important prisoner. The facts were told by Folger as follows:

> While charging in the edge of the town and getting separated from my regiment I was made a prisoner by Lieutenant Colonel William H. Paine, commanding the 2nd North Carolina cavalry, and was being taken to the rear. On the main road, just outside of the town, was situated a tannery, the vats of which were under cover and very close to the street.
>
> I was walking along beside the colonel's orderly and as we came near these tannery vats I saw a carbine lying on the ground. When I came up to it I quickly took it. Seeing it was loaded I fired and killed Paine's horse, which, in its death struggle, fell over towards the vats, throwing Paine head first into one of them, the colonel going completely under the tanning liquid.
>
> Seeing that the colonel was safe enough for the moment I turned my attention to his orderly, who, finding his pistol had fouled and was useless, was about to jump his horse over the fence to the right and escape that way if he could, but not being able to do so, concluded he had better surrender. The reason I did not fire upon him was that the last shot in the captured carbine was fired at the colonel's horse. As the orderly did not know this, it was my play to make him think instant death awaited him if he attempted escape. So I took him in and disarmed him, and made him help to get the colonel out of the tanning liquid.
>
> His gray uniform, with its white velvet facing, his white gauntlet gloves, face and hair, had all become completely stained so that he presented a most laughable sight.
>
> I then mounted the orderly's horse, and marched them before me to the market place, where I turned them over to the

authorities, who laughed heartily at the comical predicament of the colonel. I had been captured by Colonel Paine's command the winter before, and you can just believe that I was glad to return the compliment with interest.

A Perfect Fit

In 1867 an ex-Confederate recalled this incident which more than likely was a common occurrence in the early days of the campaign.

On the second invasion of Pennsylvania, which terminated in the defeat of the Confederates upon the plains of Gettysburg, one corps of the grand old army penetrated to Carlisle, and, while on the march from there to Gettysburg, the following scene took place.

Crowds of country people had flocked to the wayside to gaze upon the Johnnies; among them not a few were stalwart lads, who, dressed in their best, and with their girls by their sides, were peculiarly the object of Johnnies' wit. Whether it was envy because Johnnie had no gal, or contempt for men who might be serving their country instead of the ladies, I've a shrewd suspicion but I shan't say.

A fine looking soldier of a North Carolina regiment, barefooted and ragged, had dragged his tender pedals over many weary miles without a murmur, but finding his comrades fast leaving him in the rear, called to the Corps Commander as he was passing, and begged permission to relieve his necessitous condition from the well-shod country people. The General consented that he might take one pair of shoes.

The soldier walked up to one of the aforesaid lads, surrounded by a bevy of gaily dressed girls, and accosted him thus: 'I say, mister, come up out of those boots, I must have 'em.' Citizen replied, 'but your General has issued orders that private property must be respected.' Soldier. 'If that is a No. 9 you are wearing you had better come out of it. If you want to argue the case, you must do it with old Bal, (his musket) who never speaks but once. So out with you.'

The citizen reluctantly drew off his boots and passed them over to the soldier, who wrapping his dusty pants about his legs, drew 'em on tops out, and asking the former proprietor how he liked the fit, he resumed his march amid the shouts of comrades, and with the girls smiling at their lover's sad plight.

"Pig Out"

A Confederate soldier from Statesville, North Carolina, told the following humorous story:

Just before the battle of Gettysburg the 4th North Carolina Regiment was on picket duty near Carlisle, Pa. The band of that regiment was encamped near one of those fine Dutch barns, around which were several hog houses about six feet square with a hole in one side just large enough for a hog to go in and out, while a few chickens were scratching for a living. It was suggested that they were contraband of war. Nat said: 'This is an enemy's country, and we have a perfect right to confiscate those chickens.' Bob by this time had one at full run, and Charley was heading it off from the gate; and as it turned the corner of the barn, Bob was just tipping its tail when it darted into a hog house. Bob didn't take time to see whether a hog was in it or not; but as he started in an old sow started out, and both were in a hurry and they wedged in the door tight. Bob kicked his heels high to keep them out of the hog's mouth and held his head high to keep her tail out of his mouth. Finally the hog wiggled out and let Bob down. He looked up reproachfully and said: 'Charley, why didn't you help me?' Charley replied sympathetically: 'I was afraid de old sow'd bite me.'

Plenty of Plunder

It happened that a member of the Fourth Texas came into the camp of the Texas Brigade after dark on the 30th of June. He wrote:

Rejoining the brigade . . . at its camp near Chambersburg, and being very tired, I lay down near the wagons and went to sleep. Awakened next morning . . . I witnessed not only an unexpected but a wonderful and marvelous sight. Every square foot of an acre of ground not occupied by a sleeping or standing soldier, was covered with choice food for the hungry . . .

The sleepers were the foragers of the nights, resting from their arduous labors – the standing men, their mess-mates who remained as camp-guards and were now up to their eyes in noise, feathers and grub. Jack Sutherland's head pillowed itself on a loaf of bread, and one arm was wound caressingly half-around a juicy-looking ham. Bob Murray, fearful that his captives would take to their wings or be purloined had wound the string, which bound half a dozen frying chickens around his right big toe; one of [Haywood] Brahan's widespread legs was embraced by two overlapping crocks of apple-butter and jam, while a tough old gander, gray with age, squawked complainingly at his head without in the least disturbing his slumber. Dick Skinner lay flat on his back – with his right hand holding to the legs of three fat chickens and a duck, and his left, to those of a large turkey – fast asleep and snoring in a rasping bass voice that chimed in well with the music of the fowls . . .

The scene [was] utterly indescribable and I shalt make no further attempt to picture it.

Adams County's Loss

In 1982, Kathleen Georg Harrison, who is currently Chief Historian at the Gettysburg National Military Park, took time to read through all of the Pennsylvania state "damage claims" filed by residents of Adams County shortly after the Civil War. The claims were mostly submitted in 1868 in order to recover damages caused by the Union and Confederate armies as they roamed and plundered the countryside during the Gettysburg Campaign of 1863. One should remember however, that the figures below do not reflect claims made by many county citizens to the *Federal* government for similar damages.

Quoting Ms. Harrison:

After a perusal of the State Damage Claim applications, a general breakdown of *large* items taken by Confederates can be made:

at least 800 horses

at least 1,000 head of cattle
about a dozen mules
over 200 hogs
over 400 sheep all driven off from Adams County
also about 100 wagons, 90 wagon beds, and 50
buggies and carriages were taken . . .

The total summary of real and personal property came to about $552,383 in this county. The highest loss occurred in Franklin County, just to the east, which lost $838,162 during the invasion. The reader must note that Ms. Harrison did not list the literally thousands of smaller household items, or the hundreds of acres of growing crops or the tons of stored harvests taken or destroyed. These claims files are endless but fascinating inventories of missing items such as watches, knives, shoes, hats, clothes (male and female), toothbrushes, plows, canned preserves, sleigh bells, bedsheets, library books, county maps, weapons, dried fish, money, jewelry, medical supplies, house furniture, lanterns, tools (especially blacksmith), toys – in short, everything that literally was not nailed down and that a soldier could take in a knapsack, haversack, wagon or on horseback.

Spies

Prior to almost any invasion into enemy territory, a good army commander will usually send out advance scouts or spies to locate roads, river fords, bridges, friendly civilians, his adversary's movements and positions, and the like. So it was before and during the Gettysburg Campaign. Here is how some Adams County citizens remembered these little-known and sinister figures who skirt the fringes of military history.

Sarah B. King, living on York Street, was witness to some of the first Rebels to arrive in the town. She said they were guided by a "spy" of sorts as she penned this interesting recollection:

It was said that a man who once worked at blacksmithing in Gettysburg was one of those who piloted them and it was reported that this same man went to the home of Adam Doersom, Sr., and made a demand for money and even tortured the man who had befriended him, for this same fellow had worked for Mr. Doersom years before that time and lived [with] his family, worthy people who were kind to all. The town was very indignant over the reports. . . .

When General Early's Confederates of Ewell's Corps entered the town, John Wills, the son of J. Charles Wills who operated the Globe Inn hotel, noticed a Rebel officer whom he remembered.

[When] the second company came up Chambersburg street [I saw] at the head of it . . . a big man with long hair, a striking figure. The minute I saw him I recognized him. I went closer to

28

him and finally as they moved toward York street I went to the hotel and called my father out and asked him whether the big man hadn't staid at our hotel three or four weeks prior. The man finally saw us looking at him . . . [and] turned his face to the other side of the street. . . .

He had come to the Globe Inn and remained there over night. His ostensible purpose was to try to sell us a recipe . . . but asked us a number of questions about the roads and location of other taverns in the county and the Cumberland Valley.

Wills explained how the stranger had stayed up far into the night writing notes in his room by the light of a single candle. Young Wills also mentioned that he encountered "Jim Furley" who was with the Rebels. Furley was the man who stayed with the Adam Doersom family to learn the blacksmith trade. He told Wills that he tried to capture the telegraph equipment in Gettysburg, but was foiled when the operator, Hugh D. Scott, escaped with the apparatus to Hanover.

Sue Myers, another Gettysburg civilian, also made a statement concerning this man, Furley. On June 26, during the Rebel advance, she left her school on the Chambersburg Pike and took shelter inside the Eagle Hotel. Later that day, Myers and her friends "watched the Rebels ride into town, led by an old resident of the town, who had become a rebel."

On June 29, after Early's Division had left, four Union soldiers of Company C, Cole's Maryland Cavalry, entered Gettysburg and stopped at the Eagle Hotel. (One of these soldiers was Samuel N. McNair.) While at the hotel, the troopers had quite an adventure. A reporter for the Emmitsburg *Chronicle* explains:

A little while after a stranger in citizens dress passed by. The soldiers remarked a peculiar military bearing about the stranger that indicated he was a soldier. Although the other members of the party opposed, McNair started in pursuit and being better mounted gained on the man who was making every effort to get away. Shots were exchanged between the two, the stranger shooting rapidly. McNair [shot] frequently enough to draw the other's fire. When the young Union soldier judged that the other had spent his ammunition he spurred his horse and captured him. The man proved to be a 'Johnnie' but when he surrendered he said he was a chaplain. McNair replied, 'Yes, a fighting chaplain, evidently from the way in which you are armed and your manner of using your gun.'

Interestingly, that morning McNair had captured a Confederate cavalryman entering Gettysburg from the west. The man carried dispatches from Lee to Ewell. And later that day McNair caught a third Rebel near Bream's Tavern west of town on Marsh Creek. This unfortunate soul happened to be an artilleryman who was hunting for whiskey.

PART II

The Battle: July 1, 1863

The Fighting Blacks

One of the most compelling things I have ever read regarding the Battle of Gettysburg was this one sentence found in the July 24, 1863, edition of the New York *Herald.* Under the title "Incidents of the Battle" it says:

"Washington, July 10, 1863

Among the rebel prisoners who were marched through Gettysburg there were observed seven negroes in uniform and fully accoutred as soldiers."

If this report is true, and it very likely is, it remains easily as a most fascinating mystery of the Civil War. Could it be possible that somewhere in the hundreds of thousands of men who served the Confederacy, that a squad or even a company of blacks was actually enlisted to fight for the South?

Most people are aware that very late in the War many Southerners, including Robert E. Lee, advanced this very idea. It would come as no surprise to find that it was already happening in a limited way even earlier in the war.

The Daring Cavalryman

Surgeon Abner Hard of the 8th Illinois Cavalry, whose regiment was one of the first units to make contact with Rebel forces on July 1, stated in a history of that unit in 1868:

> About eleven o'clock a.m., General Reynolds and staff arrived on the ground, and soon after, the advance of his corps. As they came upon Seminary Ridge and deployed in line the cavalry was withdrawn. General Buford told me that he never saw so daring and successful a thing as was done by one of the Eight Illinois men. As the cavalry skirmishers fell back, one man, either not hearing the command or determined not to yield, at first stood his ground, then lay down in the grass until the enemy's line was nearly upon him, when he arose and cried out at the top of his voice, 'Come on – we have them.' Whether the rebels were astonished at his madness, or thought he was an officer leading on a host, we know not, but their line faltered; just then a regiment of General Reynolds corps filed in through the woods behind the rebel line, cutting them off from support, and in this manner we were enabled to capture General Archer and his brigade numbering about eight hundred men.

Official sources list 432 total missing and prisoners in Archer's brigade during the campaign.

Sisters and Brothers

These two interesting "family" reunions took place during and right after the battle. They must have brightened the lives of four people faced with so much horror and suffering around them.

Mary Horner, a citizen of the town, witnessed the first.

> We were watching the coming in of Archer's brigade as prisoners [on July 1] when Mrs. Mary Carson, wife of the cashier of the bank, [T. Duncan], asked us into her house . . . [on York Street]. Mrs. C. proposed that we should go to the vault of the bank –which we did – nineteen women and children, two dogs and a cat. While in these close quarters a message came that Lieutenant Charles Hunt, of the 5th Maine Battery, was at the door wounded. He was a brother of Mrs. C., who ordered him to be taken to the cellar, and there lying on a piano box, Dr. Horner extracted the bullet from his leg and cared for his wound.

Another who recalled the reuniting of Mrs. Carson and Lieutenant Hunt was Lieutenant Charles A. Fuller, 61st New York Infantry, who after being wounded on July 2, was taken to the Carson home.

> I was taken to the house of Mr. Carson. . . . When I was deposited at his house, Mr. Carson was in Philadelphia to get and return the bank's property, but Mrs. Carson was there, and, if I had been a near relative, she could not have done more to make my stay tolerable. As an instance of the romance in war the following occurred. Mrs. Carson's brother was an officer in a Maine battery. He was in the first day's engagement and was quite seriously wounded. He managed to get to his sister's house, I believe he was not disturbed by the Rebels, and left for his home the day before I came.

The second meeting was recorded by Mother Regina, one of the Sisters of Charity who came to Gettysburg to assist in nursing the wounded. She wrote:

"While going over a field encampment we found the brother of one of our Sisters. He had been wounded in the chest and in the ankle. His kind officer allowed him to be removed to the hospital in which his sister was stationed. The brother and sister had not met for nine years."

The nun was Serena Klimkiewicz. Her soldier brother was Thaddeus – and both had a famous ancestor. He was the Polish general Thaddeus Kosciusko, who had become an American hero in the Revolutionary War by helping the United States in the fight against England.

The Choice

In 1944 during the height of World War II and eighty-one years after the Battle of Gettysburg, Mrs. Rosa A. (Snyder) Gettle was spoken of as the only

31

person living in that year who had then been a civilian in the town during the famous three-day battle.

In 1863, Rosa Snyder had been a little girl a year or so shy of entering school. She lived with seven other children and her mother, Catherine, in a house on Baltimore Street where it turned into the Turnpike of that same name. Rosa's father, Conrad Snyder, a farmer, had died in 1860.

On July 1, during the rapidly approaching fighting, Mrs. Snyder took her children down the pike to the house of a friend named Benner. Soon they were ordered out of the house by Federal officers. Once again the family headed south, where they stopped and rested at another farmhouse. A newspaper reporter sums up Mrs. Gettle's story.

> It was while there that they were joined by their thirteen-year-old brother, John. He had been staying with a farmer in the neighborhood. With the battle approaching, the farmer and his family had fled and left John to watch over the house. As the combat came nearer, John, too, decided to leave.
>
> On the way through the woods to the farmhouse where his brother and sisters were, John met a soldier. John was wearing a ring belonging to the farmer's wife which the soldier wanted. John refused to give up the ring. The soldier told him to give up the ring or to give up his coat and trousers. John took his choice and arrived at the farmhouse in his drawers.

Naughty Jack

Captain John Cook, 80th New York Infantry, told of an amusing sight he experienced on July 1 while his company laid down in the grass near McPherson's Ridge waiting for the enemy to strike.

> It must have been along in the early afternoon when Lieutenant [John M.] 'Jack' Young came in from the left skirmishing company to report. Jack was a character. He had served as a sergeant in the Mexican War and a field-piece captured at Cerro Gordo still bears as a trophy his name as one of the captors. High-spirited and insensible to fear, as an officer he had but one fault. He would get drunk and when drunk was riotous. There was a verse of a bawdy ballad, which, when in that condition, he used to sing, or, rather, shout with the voice of a Stentor. He had been put in arrest for an escapade as we passed through Washington, but at his earnest petition had been released to share in the action. He was too good a man in a fight to be left out.
>
> The excitement acted on him like a stimulant, and as he came up along the front of the line of men lying down almost rigidly nervous under the prolonged exposure, with shot and shell whistling around him, he roared out the utterly unrepeatable verse of his favorite ballad at the top of his voice, and, raising his cap and wiping his heated face, shouted, 'Colonel, it's damned hot out

there.' The whole line broke into a roar of laughter, and the cool insouciance of Jack did more to relieve the mental strain which the long waiting under fire had caused than anything else could have done.

Lieutenant Young was dismissed from the service in 1864. Evidently someone in command at that time did not have a sense of humor when it came to dealing with "Naughty Jack."

A Perfect Shot

Captain Hubert Dilger, commander of Battery I, 1st Ohio Light Artillery, by 1863, was known throughout the army as one of the finest artillerymen on either side. His conduct at Chancellorsville would win him a Medal of Honor. Dilger claimed to have been a German Army artillery officer who was born in Baden, Germany, in 1836. At any rate, no matter what he had done prior to the war, he had certainly found a home in the Eleventh Corps of the Army of the Potomac. His capability was proved once again on July 1. An eyewitness in the 157th New York Infantry wrote:

> The [units of the Eleventh Corps] passed through the town to a point a few hundred yards north of it, where three roads come together. The Mummasburg road branching to the northwest; the Carlisle road to the north, and the Harrisburg Road to the northeast. . . . the 157th regiment being posted in a field on the right of the First Corps, with the . . . First Ohio Battery . . . immediately in its front. The shells from the guns of the enemy [on Oak Hill] flew over the battery and fell in the regiment, doing much injury. . . . The first shot from the Ohio Battery flew over the Confederate battery. At this the rebels were jubilant and yelled in derision. Captain Dilger now sighted the gun and fired it. The shot dismounted a rebel gun and killed the horses. Captain Dilger tried it a second time, sighting and firing the gun. No effect being visible with the naked eye, Colonel Brown [of the 157th] who was near, asked 'What effect, Captain Dilger?' [The] captain after looking through his glass, replied, 'I have spiked a gun for them, plugging it at the muzzle.'

Interestingly enough, on July 2 a wounded and captured Union soldier, J. M. Silliman, of the 17th Connecticut Infantry, who was a prisoner in a Confederate field hospital just in rear of Oak Hill, wrote:

"I saw a rebel cannon which had been struck in its mouth by one of our shots and flattened out."

Whether it was the same gun is impossible to know, but it is most certainly a strange and curious coincidence.

Coincidence or not, one other person noticed just such a cannon while visiting the Gettysburg area on July 7. This sightseer was Jacob Hoke of

Chambersburg, PA, who said:

"Returning to town [after rambling over the field of battle] we saw at the depot three or four Disabled cannon. They were broken in various ways. One had been struck squarely in the muzzle by a solid shot one size larger than its calibre. The ball stuck fast in the muzzle and broke a piece out of it."

John Snyder's Run

Reuben Ruch, Company F, 153rd Pennsylvania Infantry, recalls a humorous sight he witnessed during the Union army's retreat on July 1.

Everybody has heard of Jake Snyder's ride, but nobody has heard of John Snyder's run, or retreat, at Gettysburg. We had an old fellow in the company by the name of John Snyder, whom nobody supposed could be moved to go faster than a walk. He was hard of hearing, and being too slow for drill, he was used for doing the chores about camp. But he always carried a gun. He was good enough to go into battle, for he could stop a bullet as good as anybody. Just as I came out of the woods I looked toward where the battery had been posted on the hill and I saw John Snyder in full retreat, with his head drawn down behind his knapsack and his heels flying. He was the only man in our company that I saw running at Gettysburg.

Face Down

When the battle opened on Wednesday, the first of July, a North Carolina regiment found itself in the thick of the fighting near the Mummasburg Road northwest of Gettysburg. Moving forward, the colonel of the regiment, surveying the situation, "beheld a human head, face downward, flat on the earth. Calling out, 'Hello! who's that,' the head cautiously emerged from the short grass and disclosed the features of a member of his regiment, rather suspected of a 'hankerin for the rear' at times. 'Why John, poor fellow, where are you hit, and is it dangerous?' says the Colonel.

'Well, no where in particular jist yit, Colonel, but I think I'll git over it,' was the reply of the *he-row*, as he buried his face in the grass again! He recovered."

A Fight Unfought

Anger took the place of common sense in one small portion of the Confederate army on July 1. Even while the Battle of Gettysburg was in progress, two Southern "gentlemen" could only concentrate on each wanting to kill the other. This is how it happened:

Captain George V. Moody commanded a Louisiana artillery battery in Alexander's battalion. His comrade-in-arms, Captain Pichegru Woolfolk, led a Virginia battery. Both men had quarreled over the fact that one or the other had usurped the other's place in the order of march of the artillery column. The argument quickly got out of hand; Moody challenged Woolfolk to a duel which was to take place on the morning of July 2, using infantry rifles at ten paces. However, the duel had to be postponed on July 2, because of the pressing activities of the artillery battalion in preparing for an attack on the Union lines that afternoon.

Fortunately, it never did take place. Captain Woolfolk was wounded in the battle, and the two men never saw each other again. By the time Woolfolk returned to the army, Captain Moody had been captured in Tennessee where he remained a prisoner until the end of the war.

Both officers met unusual fates. Moody, an attorney, was killed by a man he prosecuted in Port Gibson, Mississippi. Woolfolk died when a portion of the ceiling of the Virginia state capitol fell, crushing him into eternity.

Captain Irsch's Last Stand

The Eleventh Corps of the Army of the Potomac did not have the best reputation in that army. In fact, after the Northern defeat at Chancellorsville two months before, their standing in the army was at a very low ebb indeed. And much has been written about the Eleventh's actions in the first day's fight at Gettysburg – how it was the first to retreat, uncovering the right flank of the First Corps, and so on. However, the following example of courage and spirit by a *German* officer of the Eleventh and how he won the Medal of Honor at Gettysburg, will go far to show that not all of that corps were "fleet of foot."

In 1863 Captain Francis Irsch commanded Company D, 45th New York Infantry, part of the Third Division, (General Carl Schurz) of that ill-fated corps. Arriving on the field about eleven o'clock a.m. in advance of the Eleventh Corps and after a double-quick march of several miles, part of the 45th was immediately ordered to relieve some of the cavalry units which were slowly retiring before General Heth's Confederate division. As he moved forward, Irsch came in contact with a force of Alabama sharpshooters and two Rebel batteries planted on Oak Hill. Finding cover, Irsch's unit waited for reinforcements. However, General Ewell, seeing the small number of Union soldiers, ordered two brigades to dash ahead and break the weak Federal line. Captain Irsch discovered this movement and advised Dilger's battery, which immediately opened a terrible fire on the Southerners. The 12th and 13th Massachusetts Infantry regiments, posted along Oak Ridge and the Mummasburg Road, added musket fire to the barrage. Soon after this, Irsch ordered a charge, which drove O'Neal's Alabama brigade back into the two Massachusetts regiments, causing the loss of a large part of three regiments of O'Neal's brigade. Another portion of this brigade fortified itself inside in a nearby barn, which Irsch later stormed, capturing about one hundred more prisoners.

When the retreat of the First and Eleventh Corps was finally ordered later in the day, the captain and his small battalion found themselves caught up in the throng of broken commands attempting to reach the safety of Cemetery Hill, south of Gettysburg. Captain Irsch's men stayed together until they reached Chambersburg Street where they took possession of a block of houses and kept up an incessant fire on the victorious Confederates who were slowly but surely taking over the town and making prisoners of thousands of Union soldiers.

Soon, there were no less than six hundred Federals barricaded in the block held by Irsch. Their stubborn defense here lasted several hours. About sundown, one source reported,

> . . . the Confederates demanded the surrender of the gallant little band. Captain Irsch was permitted to leave the temporary defense under a flag of truce and satisfy himself that no succor was in sight and that further resistance was useless. . . . After a consultation with the other officers, the men were ordered to destroy their arms and ammunition and surrender. Captain Irsch was sent to Libby Prison. He made one escape, was recaptured and sent back again. . . .

For his bravery, skill, and daring intrepidity, Francis Irsch was awarded the Medal of Honor. Unfortunately, his actions that day remain an almost unknown footnote in the history of the battle.

General Lee's Critics

Just using the words "Lee" and "criticism" in the same sentence will place any writer in trouble with most Civil War readers today. Since Robert E. Lee reached god-like status even before his untimely death in October of 1870, it is not the purpose of this story to detract from his obviously excellent character. The following quotes are presented as "food for thought" and to indicate that even though Lee led a most magnanimous campaign, there were people who considered him simply an enemy and a traitor. Here are a few examples:

From Pennsylvania College Martin L. Stoever wrote this in a letter to a friend in September of 1863:

> I also heard the woman [Mary Thompson], whose house he made his headquarters, say that he [Lee] made her deliver up all the jellies and jams she had with three bottles of wine which she had herself made for medicinal purpose, without offering her any compensation. He, moreover, in her presence with an oath said that he intended to make the Yankees that day dance [on Thursday, July 2]. I agree with you in the sentiment that this wicked rebellion has so hardened and corrupted its actors that they seem to have lost all honor and principle.

Professor Michael Jacobs, also of Pennsylvania College, wrote in 1864:

> [Lee] transcended the rules held sacred amongst belligerents, [when] he ascended the college cupola, for the purpose of gaining a nearer and a more perfect view of our left center, although that building was at the time used by the [rebels] as a hospital,

and the usual flag designed to give information of that fact was floating in the breeze by his side.

George Duffield, Jr., a Michigan nurse tending the wounded, reported this incident on July 9, 1863, in a letter to his brother:

> . . . Gen. Lee . . . planted one of his heaviest batteries right behind a hospital (where some of our Michigan boys were) and of whom [stated] that he and General Rhodes [sic] directed the battle on the 2d day from the lofty cupola of the College, when the Red Hospital flag was flying.

Annie Young, who lived very near the college, expressed the same sentiments in a July 17 letter which will not be quoted here due to its redundancy.

However, Mary Thompson, mentioned above, was quoted as testifying to "the gentlemanly deportment of General Lee whilst in her house, but complains bitterly of the robbery and general destruction of her goods by some of his attendants. Of General J. E. B. Stuart, whom she saw and heard converse with Lee at her house, she gives just the opposite testimony. She describes him as a man rough in his manner and cruel and savage in his suggestions. She heard him urge upon Lee the propriety of shelling and destroying the town of Gettysburg . . . and of displaying the black flag. To all of this, General Lee is said to have replied in the negative."

Although many of Lee's officers and men refused to believe that they had been beaten at Gettysburg, some knew very well what was in the wind.

For instance, on July 4, Private E. F. Hicks of Company E, 20th North Carolina Infantry, recalled a comrade saying to him: "Hicks, I'll be damned if we ain't whipped." But more to the point of my story were the words of Lieutenant James E. Green, of Company I, 53rd North Carolina Infantry, who wrote in his diary on July 3, 1863:

> "I don't think Lee has gained anything by this fight . . . (he) fought them in their own Count[r]y on there [sic] own choice of Position, not having the means of carrying back our Wounded, and for Several other causes, I think he had better let it a loan [sic]. . . ."

Alive and Kicking

Late on Wednesday, July 1, Confederate soldiers of Steuart's brigade, Johnson's division marching from Cashtown, arrived on the battlefield. One soldier of the 2nd Maryland Infantry Battalion left this record:

> Presently we began to meet the wounded [of the first day's fight]. First a Federal in an ambulance . . . then our own. . . . [One] shot through the heart and leaning against the fence by the roadside, said to the Battalion, touched with pity as they passed him: 'Boys I'm not long for this world!'

Passing on, the division reached the vicinity of Gettysburg

before sundown. When within a mile of the place it filed to the left across a field strewn with the dead of both armies, the scene of that day's struggle. While passing over this field one of Co. A, being, like many in the division, barefooted, approached what he supposed was a dead Federal to get his shoes. Taking hold of them he was startled by the man's raising his head and saying, 'Mister, I'm not dead yet!' And so he was left undisturbed.

The Irish Thief

Richard Laracy of the 95th New York Infantry was wounded by a shell on July 1 which took off the third and fourth toe of his right foot. He hobbled into Gettysburg and took shelter on Chambersburg Street in the house of David McMillan, a single man who was a veteran of the War of 1812. Laracy explained what happened that evening:

> That night at mid-night . . . four Rebel soldiers came in to rob the wounded. They went around and asked, 'Where do you belong?' 'What state did you come from?' 'Where is your money?' 'Have you got a watch?' 'Well, fork it over.'
>
> A big red haired and red bearded Irishman came to me. 'Well, where were you born?' 'In Ireland.' 'Ireland,' said the rebel in a voice of thunder, 'and what part of Ireland,' said he in a voice more tender. 'Well,' I said, 'I was born in Kilkenny in 1844.' 'And what might be your name?' 'Richard Laracy,' said I. 'Are you related to Father Laracy of the Black Abbey?' 'Yes,' said I, 'he was my uncle.' The Rebel took up my hand and pressed it and whispered: 'Father Laracy baptized me.' 'Well,' he says, 'I wish I had met you under different circumstances.' 'But,' he says, 'I won't go through your pockets. I cannot.' . . . he drew out a big black bottle of whiskey. I took a generous pull. 'Take more,' said he, 'it will make you sleep and forget the pain – I hope we will meet again some time – Good-bye.'

PART III

The Battle: July 2, 1863

Old Ginger Fingers

An artilleryman told the following story:

> The artillery fire at Gettysburg was simply magnificent. I was in an Ohio battery, posted on Cemetery Hill. We were running short of ammunition, when General [George G.] Meade [commander of the Army of the Potomac], dismissing his staff below, rode with a single orderly to our exposed position. The boys were all at white heat and in a state of frenzy because the ammunition called for had not come. They heard the quiet man on horseback say repeatedly to the captain that the hill must be held at all hazards, ammunition or no ammunition. This vexed them, but they knew that the officer, whoever he was, spoke the truth, and they began to collect the unexploded shells that had

been fired at them from the Confederate batteries.

There were a great many of those scattered over our part of the hill, and, when Meade comprehended what the boys were doing he was greatly pleased. He dismounted and in a quiet sort of way proceeded to supervise the collection of shells. He was in fatigue dress and wore no shoulder straps, and none of them recognized him. They thought he was some ordnance officer, and finally, when he turned his horse over to his orderly and proceeded to carry shells himself, they did not resent his supervision. As a rule the shells were heavier than the General expected, and he did not compare in efficiency with the stalwart artillerymen rushing about with the recklessness and energy of madmen.

John Snicker was one of the best men in the battery, but was rough in speech and action. Seeing, as he supposed, a lieutenant or captain from the outside stooping to pick up a shell, he pushed the officer aside with the remark: 'Get out of this, old Ginger Fingers! Your mind's willin', but your body's weak, and you are in the way.' Meade, surprised and amused, stood aside. A few minutes later General Warren and staff rode up for a conference with Meade, and the cat was out of the bag.

Snicker was so overwhelmed with confusion that he almost had a fit. The sergeant tried to comfort him with the assurance that General Meade would excuse informality under such circumstances, but John insisted that what scared him was that he never came so near kicking a man in his life without doing it as he did General Meade when he stooped to pick up that shell. He was grieved to think that he hadn't recognized Meade, and was in a panic whenever he thought about what might have happened had he acted on the impulse and kicked the General commanding the army.

Dressed to Kill

Sallie P. Horner who lived in Fayetteville, Pennsylvania, during the Gettysburg Campaign, visited relatives forty years later in Nevada, Iowa, (Story County), and was interviewed by the town's local newspaper. In that article which appeared in July, 1907, Miss Horner recalled a curious little story about a great-aunt who resided in Gettysburg during those fateful days of July, 1863.

The great-aunt was very old and had to be watched over and cared for by a nurse who stayed with the family on Chambersburg Street. It is possible that Sallie's aunt may have been a member of Dr. Robert Horner's household, although she does not say this. Horner's residence sat on that street near the northeast corner of Washington Street. On the south side of Chambersburg Street was a "hat workshop" owned and operated by Smith S. McCreary. Miss Horner completed the tale in this way:

. . . in the middle of the forenoon of the second day [of the battle], when the balls were whizzing in every direction, [my great-aunt] escaped the vigilance of her nurse and presented herself at the millinery window of a relative a square and a half away. When remonstrated with for her imprudence, she apologized, 'Well, the bullets were bad, but I had to come. They do say that we'll have to evacuate Gettysburg today, and my bonnet strings are in such a frightful condition that I must have some new ones!'

A Dirty Trick

Cemetery Hill was one of the Army of the Potomac's strongest artillery positions during the battle. And being exposed, the artillerymen became clear targets for Confederate sharpshooters operating their mean business from various houses and public buildings in the town of Gettysburg.

During those days, Reverend T. P. Bucher rented a room in Walters' boarding house which was just west of the St. James Lutheran Church on the corner of York and Stratton Streets. He recalled an interesting story concerning one of the Rebel sharpshooters.

It seems that an artillery section on Cemetery Hill was being provoked constantly by a certain marksman who had taken a station in one of the town's church steeples. The battery commander, annoyed to wits' end, turned and sighted one of his cannons on that particular steeple. He then bade his men to run all around the cannon, turn somersaults, jump up and down, and generally act foolish.

Soon after this show, the Reb poked his head out to see what all the queer antics were about. Just then the artillery piece was fired – the shell striking just a foot above the fellow's head. Reverend Bucher said the sharpshooter came rushing down out of the steeple, "swearing he could not stand such shooting as that."

Short Sword

Captain Thomas L. Livermore was an officer in the 5th New Hampshire Infantry. During the early part of the Gettysburg Campaign he had been asked to fill a vacant staff position as chief of ambulances of the Second Army Corps. Livermore accepted and served efficiently in that position during the long and hotly-contested battle.

In his memoirs written years afterwards, the captain remembered a prank he played on a friend and fellow officer. While reading his comments it must be noted that Livermore's sword blade had been accidently broken in two, several weeks prior to this incident.

> Lieutenant [Charles A.] Hale, of my company, was serving on the staff of the brigade, and I played a practical joke on him . . . which might have resulted seriously for him if hand-to-hand encounters had been the fashion for staff officers. He still wore the leather scabbard upon his infantry sword, so I proposed to him to trade temporarily my sword with the steel scabbard, which was what staff officers usually carried, for his, saying that mine was more appropriate for him and his for me under the circumstances. He quickly embraced the offer, and without drawing my blade, which, as I have related, was broken in two pieces, he buckled it on, and as he did not draw it until he got into the battle on the 2d of July, and I did not foresee how soon he would be in battle and did not see him to effect a change, he did not discover the joke until, I think, in the presence of others, he with military grace and ferocity drew from the scabbard the piece of blade about eighteen inches long which adhered to the hilt. It was considered very funny.

Evidently, Livermore or Hale threw away the broken sword some time during or after the battle. About twenty years later, it turned up in the possession of a doctor who lived in the northeast part of Adams County. This doctor who lived about fifteen miles from Gettysburg, probably picked it up as a souvenir while on a visit to the battlefield. The blade was engraved with Livermore's name.

Marked for Death

As a soldier in Vietnam in 1967 – 1968, I found it was not uncommon to hear of officers being killed or wounded by their own men for a variety of reasons – usually cruelty or hardheaded stupidity which placed enlisted men in unreasonable danger. As you might expect, this was not the first war in which officers became targets by the very men they were leading. Here are two examples from the Battle of Gettysburg.

Matilda Pierce, a young Gettysburg girl, witnessed the following on July 2 while at the farm of Jacob Weikert on the Taneytown Road.

This forenoon another incident occurred which I shall ever remember. While the [Union] infantry were passing, I noticed a poor, worn-out soldier crawling along on his hands and knees. An officer yelled at him, with cursing, to get up and march. The poor fellow said he could not, whereupon the officer, raising his sword struck him down three or four times. The officer passed on, little caring what he had done. Some of his comrades at once picked up the prostrate form and carried the unfortunate man into the house. After several hours of hard work the sufferer was brought back to consciousness. . . . He seemed quite a young man, and was suffering from sunstroke. . . . As they were carrying him in, some of the men who had witnessed this act of brutality remarked: 'We will mark that officer for this.' It is a pretty well established fact that many a brutal officer fell in battle, from being shot other than by the enemy.

J. Howard Wert, who lived on a farm along White Run near the Baltimore Pike three miles south of town, recalled this tense scene also on July 2:

A battery was in camp in a field a hundred yards or so in the rear of my father's house. Soon after the middle of the day I had occasion to go to it for the purpose of seeing the commanding officer about some supplies obtained from the farm. I found everything in bustle preparatory to going into action.

But as I approached nearer a strange quiet settled down as all harnessing was suspended and men lately busy stood tense and silent. Right in the midst of the cannon I found two men facing each other. The one was [a lieutenant] of the battery, with drawn sword and face perfectly purple with passion.

The other wore the stripes of a corporal. He was a young man, rather tall. . . . His arms were folded across his breast.

'Will you saddle the orderly sergeant's horse?' demanded the officer in a voice hoarse with rage.

'No, Sir,' was the reply in a low but distant and very musical voice.

Down came a blow with the broad of a sword that only fury could give it.

The young man of the folded arms did not wince or give any exhibition of pain. But as I looked at his piercing black eyes, fixed and full and unwavering on the officer, I saw the most malignant expression of hate and desire for revenge that I have ever seen on a human countenance. It made me shudder then as if I stood in the presence of something infernal.

Again the question, again the quiet, 'No Sir' . . . and again the quick, ringing blow.

This was repeated three times . . . until . . . the battery . . . [was] ordered to move . . . to the front.

Before midnight a corpse was brought down the Baltimore pike and buried in the [Henry] Beitler garden, not an eighth of a mile from the position the battery had left that afternoon. The body was that of the battery's lieutenant.

How he met death I never knew. Those black eyes of hate, however, furnished a fruitful field of surmise.

One thing I do know that there were more cases than were ever known in which brutal officers in both Northern and Southern armies, received bullets that never came from the enemy's ranks.

A Good Time for Mischief

The young Gettysburg civilian, Albertus McCreary, was witness to what must have been an unusual sight on Baltimore Street during the day of Thursday, July 2.

> Once, hearing laughter outside, I looked out and saw a young boy standing in the middle of the street, throwing stones at the windows on either side and laughing loudly every time he broke a glass. Bullets were flying down the street, and every time one whizzed near him he would duck his head, laugh, and immediately renew his efforts to break windows. I saw that he was not one of the town boys, and asked the soldiers who he was. One of them said, 'Oh! that little devil followed the army up from the South.' He seemed to be having great fun breaking Yankee windows. I do not know what became of him.

Let's Buy 'Em

It was said that on the afternoon of July 2, when some of the Texans in Robertson's brigade of Hood's division were moving up toward Devil's Den against Smith's 4th New York Battery, a sergeant of one company said drearily:

"I reckon the only way to get those guns is to take 'em."

Everyone was gloomy until the company "wag," who was a stutterer, spoke up:

"I s-s-say, boys, can't we c-c-chip in 'nuff to b-b-buy the old things for spot c-c-cash?"

The grim humor of the thought tickled the waiting Confederates and many went into the attack with smiles on lips that never smiled again.

He *Felt* the Firing

Albertus McCreary, a young man living in Gettysburg at the time of the battle, told this little story about something most people take for granted. At the time, his family was living in a house at the corner of Baltimore and High Streets.

> From [July 1] until the end of the battle we were within the Confederate lines and knew nothing of the state of affairs outside. . . . Although we were confined to the house for the next two days, we only took to the cellar at intervals, when there was heavy cannonading. The vibrations could be felt, and the atmosphere was so full of smoke that we could taste saltpeter. One of our party was a deaf and dumb man, who, though he could not hear the firing, plainly felt the vibrations and could tell when the firing was heaviest as well as we. He would spell out on his finger, 'That was a heavy one.' The whizzing of the shells overhead and the sharp snap of bullets through the trees in the yard kept us well keyed up.

Rigby's Repairs

A rare but good example of "fixing under fire" was reported by Lieutenant A. N. Parsons, commander of Battery A, 1st New Jersey Light Artillery, at Gettysburg. On July 2, seeing Rigby's 1st Maryland Artillery, Battery A, open fire on Confederates in the woods near Culp's Hill, Parsons explained:

> Rigby's battery was twelve-pound [actually 3″ ordnance rifles] rifled guns. About the second shot he fired the recoil of the gun broke an axletree. I happened up about that time (General Meade was there), and told Captain Rigby to have his gun dragged down in the hollow, where my battery was, bring his traveling forge alongside of mine, behind a big rock, and with the two fires and the two smiths we could mend the axletree directly. It was done. The men welded that axletree while the shells from the enemy's batteries went screaming over their heads like wild geese in a storm. In less than one hour that axle was mended, the gun remounted, hauled back into position, and blazed away as though nothing had happened; and all this was done during the incessant roar of artillery.

This event took place on Power's Hill, a mile or so south of Cemetery Hill.

Fourteen Days

Georgia Confederate soldier, William Paul, remembered this severe experience which may rank him as the man who lay on the Gettysburg *battlefield* proper, longer than any other wounded man. It happened late on July 2 when A. R. Wright's brigade attacked Cemetery Ridge.

The 48th Georgia Regiment was in line of battle, fronting Gettysburg, and we were ordered forward. The first line of Federals was behind breastworks made of rails, from which we soon drove them under a heavy fire to that noted rock fence. By the time we reached the rock fence all the officers in Company I, 'Wilson's Tigers,' had been killed or wounded. We had seventy-three men when the fight began, and only three men escaped without a bullet piercing their bodies. I was a corporal, and led the company to within twenty yards of the rock fence, when I was shot down, and the few remaining fell back.

I remained on the battlefield fourteen days, unable to move or help myself, lying between two corn rows smeared with my own blood, until I was sunburned from head to foot, my clothes having been torn off, and two of the wounds had become fly-blown. After this we were removed from the battlefield to Baltimore, and there lay on a street for several hours. Some pitied and others reviled us. The most charitable act done for me was by a fine-looking lady, dressed in black, who gave me a fine comb, and I was not long in making my head more comfortable. If that lady is alive, I would like to send her a nice Florida present.

I was finally moved to Chester Hospital, where I had to plead with the doctors to prevent amputation of my leg. It had so decayed that the bone and leaders were visible. After a long spell of typhoid fever, I was moved to Point Lookout Prison, where I was detained for about seventeen months before being exchanged. Then a thirty days' furlough was given me. After leaving Richmond, it took the thirty days to reach home, as I was going around Sherman's army to Augusta, Ga.

I am now old, seventy-seven years of age, living at Wildwood, Fla., and have a warm place in my heart for all the old boys who wore the gray.

Pitzer's Treasure

The following intriguing tale of July 2 was related by a young Gettysburg civilian named Charles McCurdy.

There was a farmer named Pitzer living near Round Top, his farm being the scene of some of the fiercest fighting. Mr. Pitzer had no faith in paper money and had accumulated a store of gold and silver coin amounting, it was said, to some thousands of dollars. He kept this money at home, apparently having as little confidence in banks as he had in greenbacks. Whether in a moment of panic, when he found himself about to be surrounded by fighting, he hid his money in a bake oven in his yard, or whether he had adopted it before as his strong box, I do not know. . . . at all events he hid his wealth there and it was found and taken. . . . It was never recovered.

47

The Pitzer farmhouse.

In the evening of the second day's battle, a Confederate cavalryman rode up to the residence of Mr. Alexander Buehler in Gettysburg. Mr. Buehler had a drug and book store in the front room of his dwelling, which of course, was closed. He was a man of the very highest character, universally esteemed and trusted. The soldier, who carried a valise on the pommel of his saddle, inquired for him and when he appeared told him that he had been sent by General [William] Mahone, a brigade commander of the third corps, to ask him to take charge of the valise he carried until called for. Mr. Buehler consented and carried the bag, whose contents were very heavy, to his bedroom and put it under his bed. The next evening the same soldier appeared, reclaimed the bag and rode off.

Some years after the battle, Mr. Buehler told me of the incident. He was confident he had acted as General Mahone's banker in the case of poor Mr. Pitzer's hoard. Doubtless it was found impossible to guard it during the excitement of the struggle and the general had inquired for a perfectly reliable man to whom it might safely be committed, and had been assured that Mr. Buehler was such a man.

Another view of this incident was written by a sightseer to the battlefield on July 8, John B. Linn. While visiting with Joseph Sherfy near the now famous "Peach Orchard," Linn said:

Old Emmanuel Pitzer, [Sherfy's] neighbor, had died some three weeks ago leaving $5000 in gold and silver in the house, the son was warned to hide it, but neglected it until the rebel skirmishers approached when he took the bag and put it under the bake-oven. They saw him do it and of course seized the whole of it. I was telling Mr. [T. P.] Bucher about it, when he remarked he thought it was a just retribution, as the children had all been very anxious for the old man's death, and one of the daughters had gone so far as to purchase mourning clothes six months previous. The son's name is Samuel Pitzer.

One other comment was made in a short article in the Gettysburg *Compiler* in August of 1884. The reporter stated that a soldier in the 3rd Georgia Infantry (Anderson's division), named Jim Parr had found $1200 in specie under a bake oven during the battle, and gave it to a friend in the cavalry who took it south for him during the retreat. The article ended by saying it probably belonged to, "old Mr. Samuel Pitzer, now deceased."

Anderson's division did in fact occupy the area during the battle which included the Emmanuel/Samuel Pitzer farm. Mahone's brigade was part of that division.

"Rabbit Fire"

The historian of the 118th Pennsylvania Infantry published the following story in 1888.

While the regiment lay crouching for protection in its first position near the [George] Rose House, before it had yet become engaged, a rabbit, startled from its cover by the advance of McLaws' assaulting Georgians, rushed in frightened, headlong leaps towards the Union lines. Innocent of purpose to harm, he plunged in one of his aimless jumps right into the ranks and planted his cold, sharp claws firmly into the neck of a soldier who lay flat near the right of the regiment. It was too much for the poor fellow. He gave it up, and jumping to his feet, with pitiful expression, in woe-begone tones, wringing his hands in agony, announced himself a dead man; that he had been shot in the neck; that the ball had passed entirely through, and there was no hope for him. He recovered his equanimity, however, when those in the neighborhood, who had observed the cause of his trouble, received his dire announcement with the merriment it necessarily created. When informed that a poor little rabbit had innocently been the cause of his discomfiture, he sheepishly resumed his place.

General Lafayette McLaws, who remembered the rabbit between the battle lines, added this in a letter from Savannah, Georgia, in August of that same year:

"I think that, in all probability, it was the same rabbit, and perhaps it was the same one which a Confederate 'hollowed at,' saying: 'Go it, old fellow; and I would be glad to go with you, if I hadn't a reputation to sustain.'"

Pennsylvania Biscuits

Private James O. Bradfield, Company E, 1st Texas Infantry, recounted a tale about a comrade just prior to General Hood's afternoon attack on the Union lines south of Gettysburg on July 2.

> In our company was a tall, robust young fellow named Dick
> Childers, who was noted for the energy and talent he displayed
> in procuring rations. On this occasion Dick's haversack was
> well stocked with nice biscuits which a kind Dutch lady had
> given him. As we were marching by the right flank, our left sides
> were turned towards the enemy. A shell from the mountain [i.e.
> the Union lines] in front struck the ground near our batteries,
> and came bouncing along across the field, and as Dick hap-
> pened to be just in the line of fire, it struck him, or rather, his

haversack, fairly, and scattered biscuits all over that end of Pennsylvania. But the strange part of it is, that it did not knock the man down, but so paralyzed him that he fell, after it had passed, and lay there unable to move a muscle. The litter bearers picked him up and laid him on a stretcher, as if he had been a log. The boys all contended, however that it was the destruction of Dick's rations, and not any shock the shell gave, that paralyzed him.

Nelson's Folly

Colonel William G. Oates narrated the following story about one of his soldiers in the 15th Alabama Infantry.

John Nelson was 23 years old when enlisted. He was an Irishman and one of his most prominent characteristics was his desire to fight. He would fight any of the men [in the regiment] personally, and would go into every battle, and when given the first opportunity would run out of it.

At Gettysburg, Captain [William J.] Bethune detailed Sergeant [Pat] O'Conner to hold Nelson to the work. When he undertook to break for the rear O'Conner collared him and held him to his place until he was killed. O'Conner was also an Irishman, and one of the bravest. Nelson died trying to flee instead of bravely facing the foe. As O'Conner let him down he said, 'Now I guess you will not run away.'

Quite a Trip

Captain Dudley Chase, 17th United States Infantry, relayed the following, which took place in the late afternoon of July 2 as the "Regular Brigade" made an attack westward from the northern face of Little Round Top.

A Lieutenant temporarily attached to my company, astonished me as we were going down the slope, silent and grim, by leaving his place in the line and running along the rear of the company yelling, 'Give 'em hell, men! give 'em hell!' Twice I ordered him to desist, telling him I was in command and to keep quiet.

When we made the run across the marsh, this Lieutenant was particularly vociferous, swinging his sword, etc., and in the center of the marsh he fell and was covered with mud. His sword scabbard had gotten between his legs and tripped him.

All who saw his misadventure laughed.

Bravery Unsurpassed

Another "Regular" of the 17th United States Infantry, J. P. Hackett, relayed a good account of true heroism which occurred on the afternoon of July 2.

Our regiment . . . took position a few rods east of the wheat-field, on a little hill. . . .

(One side was covered with thick brush, hiding the Confederates, while our side had a few large trees. We followed them a little too far, and when we saw them in the brush as thick as bees we fired a volley into the bushes and fell back near the foot of the hill and lay down.)

While here I saw an exhibition of bravery that I believe was never surpassed. Young Private Smith was wounded near the top of the hill, and lay where he fell. His brother, Orderly Sergeant of Company B, carrying an armful of blankets, went up the hill to fetch his brother back. He was shot and fell beside his young brother.

Lieut. [Frank E.] Stimpson, a son of an ex-Governor of Massachusetts, and a college chum of Sergt. Smith, walked fearlessly up the hill. Six feet tall, with the form of an Apollo, and a handsome face that could not be improved, the most democratic 'Regular Army' officer I ever knew. He reached the wounded brothers, took one in his arms and carried him down the hill. Then as fearlessly walked back, took the other and brought him back with never a shot fired at him.

Truly those Confederates honored a brave man.

"Stimpson's Hill," as I like to call it, can easily be visited today on the Gettysburg National Military Park. Stimpson, himself, was killed ten months later in Virginia. Sergeant Ransom Smith died of his wounds on July 26.

"Stimpson's Hill" from the northeast.

A Trick of the Mind

While retreating from his artillery position at Devil's Den in the late afternoon of July 2, Captain James E. Smith, of the 4th New York Independent Battery had a numbing experience which proves once again the old adage, "mind over matter."

A few minutes before leaving [our] last position my horse was killed which led to a ludicrous incident at my expense. . . . Lieutenant Goodman, seeing that I was without a mount, kindly gave me the use of his horse so that I might reach the head of the column then moving through the woods. While moving back . . . one of the men caught me by the leg, exclaiming, 'Captain, you're shot!'

Glancing down I saw that [my] boot was covered with blood, and located the supposed wound in the calf of the right leg. The limb began to pain, and I plainly felt the blood running into the boot. I moved my toes and the red liquid swashed between them. The foot and the limb were much swollen, I imagined, and I became anxious to ascertain the extent of the damage. . . . Calling one of the men to assist in drawing off the boot (scolding him for causing, unnecessarily, extra pain by his carelessness, while doing so) I patiently and calmly resigned myself to the inevitable. The boot being removed, and no sign of blood found, I quickly glanced at the man who had drawn it and saw on his face a broad grin. . . .

Searching for an explanation, it was discovered that the horse was shot in the flank, and by spurring, the boot-leg had come in contact with the blood which flowed from the wound.

Imagination accomplished the rest.

Yankee "Pone"

George Pile, a Confederate in the 37th Virginia of Steuart's brigade, Johnson's division, told a humorous story which probably took place on July 2.

During the Pennsylvania campaign, Dr. Matt Butler, assistant surgeon of our regiment, had a horse shot from under him and the bullet in passing through the animal's body left a bad wound in his foot. He was limping along the road in company with a wounded companion and a negro hospital helper. 'Look hear, I'se got to git you folks to a safe place, de Yankees is comin' an' deys comin' close. I'se got to hide you, I tell you I is,' said the negro.

They walked on as fast as they could and soon passed through a spring house lot. A woman was there baking a large pone of cornbread by an open fire which smelled mighty good to these hungry men. They told her they were very hungry and would like to have something to eat. She told them she would like to give them some food but that she had none except what she was baking and she was preparing that for a Yankee Colonel, calling his name.

They left her and when they came across a thickly wooded hillside the negro looked around and found them a good place to hide. 'Now Doctah, you got a gold dollah, give it to me, I'se gwine out to git some eatins.' He had not been gone so very long when he returned with that cornbread dripping with butter and besides a gallon of buttermilk.

'How in the world did you get it, Jim?' asked the doctor.

'I des told dat lady, de kunnel am waitin' for his pone.'

California Cake

One of the prisoners taken by the Rebels on July 1 was Rufus P. Northrop, 90th Pennsylvania Infantry. He, among others, was escorted to the rear and placed under guard. All of the Union prisoners were extremely hungry and thirsty, and were finally given a handful of flour and a bit of bacon late on July 2.

Northrop had a friend named Sutton, who had been one of the "49ers" during the California gold rush of that year. He told Northrop he could make a hoecake like they used to make in California if Northrop could get some water. Northrop slipped away and was able to fill about one half of a canteen at a nearby spring. This is what happened next:

. . . when I got [back] the men grabbed my canteen and helped themselves, but I managed to save enough to mix the batter. Sutton had fried the bacon for shortening, found an old broken crock to mix the batter and a flat shale stone and a couple of pieces of rails completed the outfit. The batter was poured on the stone while the crowd stood around and watched Sutton manipulate the savory cake. He had turned it several times, and it was taking on a tempting rich brown [color] – (my, but it smelled good) . . . from a Union battery suddenly there was an explosion [a shell had landed in the fire] and when the dust had cleared away all that was left of our California cake, was little pieces of dough and bits of stone.

The crowd set up a yell, and poor Sutton turned sadly away, remarking that swearing could not do the subject justice.

Retread!

The 123rd New York Infantry Regiment was sent to the left of the Union line late on Thursday, July 2. Sergeant Henry C. Morhous remembered:

[Our men] were ordered to the rear of Round Top, . . . to support the forces there engaged. The shells from the Rebel guns struck all around them in their march there, but no one was wounded. Here and there they passed a dead soldier. Down a hill, away in front of them, came tearing what they supposed was a battery, believing from this manoeuvre that our forces had been pressed back, but on a nearer approach it proved to be a Dutch sergeant of artillery going to the rear for ammunition with his caissons. As he dashed by he yelled out, 'Dis ish nod a retread, dis ish nod a retread!' The boys were very glad it was 'nod a retread,' and pressed forward. . . .

"Praying Joe" Richardson

During actual combat every soldier reacts in his own particular way. Some yell, others curse, and many just talk softly or pray to themselves. Sergeant James A. Wright, Company F, 1st Minnesota Infantry, wrote in a memoir about a man who, with some difficulty, did all three.

July 2 – . . . we were running to the right, to close the break in the lines, it was a case of 'get there' and each one was trying to make it as quickly as possible and there was not much regard to formation. I could only recall afterwards that 'Joe' Richardson was just to my right and trying to talk as we ran; but his impediment of speech, the excitement and the effort of running, to say nothing of the noise, were pretty effective hindrances. Just then I was conscious of coming in contact with something. I was then partly turned aside, staggered, confused . . . when the affair was nearly over I again saw Joe, and he was still trying to talk, and with not much better success. He was evidently trying to combine some of his unique 'swear-words' with quotations from the Bible and ancient literature, and in that way do justice to the occasion, but it did not run together very smoothly.

This is a specimen of what he was saying and a suggestion of the way he said it: 'By the l-l-lovely l-l-little angels a-and th-the g-gr-great h-ho-horn s-sp-spoon, we we'll sh-sh-show 'em th-th-there is a God in Is-Is-Israel. We-we are g-get-getting s-s-some s-s-sa-satis-faction now; ain't we sa-sargeant?'

Joe evidently was a pious man, but he could also be a cold-blooded marks-man. Sergeant Wright recalled that as they were running, Joe was loading and capping his musket. Moments later Richardson shot a Rebel who *he said* was about to fire an artillery piece at the attacking Union regiment.

He is There

Sergeant Frank B. Nickerson was wounded on the afternoon of July 2 and was carried back to a hospital of the Second Corps near Round Top where he was laid beside many desperately injured men. On his left was a Confederate he described as,

a mere boy . . . not more than seventeen years old; death's pallor was on his brow and the blood flowing from his mouth. . . . Dr. [H. M.] McAbee seemed touched with his youthful appearance and disquietude of mind, and said to him, 'My poor fellow, you cannot be helped; you can live but a little time.'

The boy broke out in a despairing cry, 'My poor mother, what will she do? I cannot die, I cannot die. She will never know what became of me. I was shot on the skirmish line and no one knows it.'

The surgeon wrote into his notebook, his name as a member of a Georgia regiment, and his mother's address, and promised, if possible to write to his mother. . . .

Twenty-two years have passed and I still have a tender memory . . . of that man that night. Last summer, in visiting the battlefield, I rode to the barn, noticed the bloodstains upon its sills, and asked the owner if any Confederates were brought here. He replied, 'Yes, one boy – and I buried him across that little rolling by the fence. I miss the place when I plow. He is there.'

Hog's Heaven

What must have been a very horrifying experience happened to Lieutenant Berzilla J. Inman, of the 118th Pennsylvania Infantry, on the night of July 2 as he lay wounded in a wooded area of the battlefield near the famous "Wheatfield." Lieutenant Inman said:

Lieutenant [James P.] Wilson and myself were wounded, and I lay upon the field until the morning of the 4th, when some of the men of Company F, of which I was an officer, carried me off on a stretcher to the hospital, where Dr. [Joseph] Thomas operated on me. On Thursday night, whilst lying within the rebel lines, the 139th [Pennsylvania] Regiment came to where I was, and I quietly called one of the sergeants and asked him to help me into our lines. He reported to the colonel the fact of being within the enemy's line, [who] immediately ordered right about face and [they] fell rapidly back, leaving me alone with the dead.

That night a number of stray hogs came to where I lay and commenced rooting and tearing at the dead men around me. Finally one fellow that in the darkness looked of enormous size approached and attempted to poke me – grunting loudly the while. Several others also came up, when, waiting my chance, I jammed my sword into his belly, which made him set up a prolonged, sharp cry. By constant vigilance and keeping from sleeping I contrived to fight the monsters off till daylight.

PART IV

The Battle: July 3, 1863

The Enterprising Irishman

This short but very interesting story appeared in a veterans' newspaper in the 1880s.

During the Battle of Gettysburg a lieutenant, the adjutant of one of the regiments in the famed Irish Brigade, was wounded and left on the field for dead. In the early morning hours of July 3 he was robbed by a member of his own regiment, an Irishman named Peter.

Later, when the adjutant was discovered to be alive, he was carried to a field hospital where he recovered from his wound. Very soon afterwards Peter went to the young lieutenant and sold him back, for five dollars, his *own* revolver which had so recently been stolen! Peter was described by the writer of this story as "a braver man never known."

He evidently was an audacious fellow, too.

Fisher's Luck

Lieutenant Rolandes E. Fisher, Company K, 5th Ohio Infantry, was running on a streak of good fortune. A thirty-one-year-old cabinetmaker from Cincinnati, Ohio, he had enlisted as a sergeant in the 5th Ohio in April of 1861, just ten days after Fort Sumter was fired upon by Confederate forces. By 1863, he had risen to the rank of first lieutenant and had been in Company K since October of 1862. Fisher had even been captured in June of 1862, but luckily was not held long; he was paroled soon afterward. By the time of the Battle of Gettysburg, Lieutenant Fisher had seen action in at least five battles including Antietam and Chancellorsville. And in the early morning of July 3, 1863, Fisher's luck was still holding out.

While checking the position of his company on that fateful day, a Rebel sharpshooter saw him standing quietly among his men in the hazy light of dawn. A shot was fired; Fisher felt the blow which knocked him to the ground. But he was not dead. Surgeon Edward Mead explained:

"The Ball entered [the] left forearm, at outer side of elbow joint passing through and making its exit at innerside at a corresponding point."

Miraculously, as the Minie' ball made "its exit at the innerside" it cut through Fisher's uniform coat and struck his pocketwatch, which stopped the flight of the deadly missile. After his recuperation, Fisher became captain of his company, and fought in the Chattanooga, Tennessee campaign, but was forced to resign in December of 1863, due to this wound.

Until his death in 1880, Captain Fisher kept the damaged watch and the smashed Confederate bullet as a reminder of a very close call at Gettysburg – on a day his luck held out.

The accompanying photograph depicts both the Confederate's bullet and the crushed watchcase which may have saved Fisher's life. Both relics were treasured by his family for many years after his death, until purchased by the author in 1977.

Lieutenant Fisher's pocket watch and the Confederate bullet that struck it.

Fireworks!

Anyone who has been in combat, or has been shot at, will tell you that any noise which sounds like gunfire will make a distinct impression on the physical and mental being of the individual. A practical joke played on a few of the Confederate invaders aptly illustrates this point.

The incident was recalled by George Frederick Neff, a Union soldier of the 24th Michigan Infantry who was slightly wounded on July 1. He was assisted to the Adams County Courthouse where he remained during the Southern occupation of the town. Early on July 3, Neff and a few of his wounded comrades noticed a Confederate brigade which had stacked their arms in the street near the courthouse and were resting prior to being ordered into a place on the fighting line.

Scouting around in the building, one of the Union soldiers had discovered a cache of firecrackers. These fireworks were all set off at once by the Yankee who was screened from the Rebels' view by the town's buildings. The Southern infantrymen jumped up, greatly startled by what sounded like rifle fire. Many seized their weapons to defend themselves.

Finally realizing what had happened, the Rebs had a good laugh over their discomfiture. Neff wrote that they believed one of their own men had set off the explosion . . . which may have relieved the embarrassment somewhat.

Almost Drafted

Young McCreary, the Gettysburg boy mentioned earlier, came very near to finding himself in a Rebel prison camp because of a blue military kepi he often wore. He narrated:

Before the battle I had been wearing my soldier's cap, but an incident occurred that led me to discard it for one of another kind until more peaceful times. I was standing on the pavement in front of our own door, watching a squad of Confederates approaching (we had lost our fear of them by this time). When they came opposite me, the officer in charge called, 'Halt!' and pointed at me.

Two of the men left the ranks, came over to me, and took me by the arms, saying, 'Come on.'

I was greatly frightened at this, and called for my father, who happened to be just inside. He at once came out, and the whole family with him, and asked what they wanted.

'He is in the army and must come with us,' they said.

Father laughed and said, 'Oh, he's only a school-boy;' but they started off with me, and it was only when a number of the neighbors, who had come out of their houses on hearing the commotion, finally persuaded them to believe I was not in the army, that they let me off.

Oh, how frightened I was! I cannot convey to any one the feeling that swept over me, as I was being led away, as I thought to a Southern prison and death.

The Million Dollar Wounds

Private William T. Simpson, a drummer in Company A, 28th Pennsylvania Infantry, was a spectator to the plight of two soldiers who were happy to be wounded near Culp's Hill on July 3. It was their ticket out of a nightmare. Simpson explains:

As we got [Sgt. McLean] into the [ambulance] [he had been wounded in the mouth], two other men were brought up. They were Sgt. Henry Shadel and Cpl. Cyrus Shenkle. Both were badly wounded. Shenkle had been hit in the head and Shadel in the shoulder. But it didn't worry them. As soon as they met, Shadel held out his hand and said to Shenkle: 'Shake! We're good for Philadelphia.'

Many years later Shenkle had an X-ray operation performed on his head and the bullet was extracted. He met me on the street one day and said: 'Wait a minute. I've got something to show you.' He put his hand down in his pocket and pulled out the bullet.

Captain Tourison's Loss

Drummer William Simpson described another incident he witnessed a few moments after the previous encounter:

> When I returned after putting McLean in the ambulance, I saw Capt. A. S. Tourison of Co. E, of the 147th [Pa] following four boys with a man in a blanket, who, I thought was wounded. Capt. Tourison formerly belonged to our regiment, and he was good to us drummer boys. We loved him. He was an old Mexican War fighter, had been in Geary's division, and was a drummer boy himself in earlier years. I went up to him with a laugh, for I was glad to see him and expected a happy greeting in return. But he just looked at me, and said: 'My poor boy is dead.' I was thunderstruck. It took all the ginger out of me. It was Will Tourison, who was the second lieutenant in his father's company. . . . I did feel sorry for Capt. Tourison. I felt as though I had met with a personal loss and I stood and watched him following the body of his boy until he was out of sight. It was the last I saw of the dear old man.

William H. Tourison, twenty-five years old and married, was wounded in the skull by a bullet on July 3 and died the same day. He was carried to the Twelfth Corps hospital on the George Bushman farm where he was buried. Young Tourison's body was later exhumed and sent home with friends on July 10.

Sergeant Hitchcock's Gift

The farm buildings of Adelina and William Bliss stood just a few hundred yards west of the Union Second Corps' position on Cemetery Ridge. Occupied off and on during the battle by Confederate sharpshooters, they became an everincreasing thorn in the side of General Alexander Hays, the commander of that part of the line. Finally, on July 3, Hays ordered the barn and house burned to prevent their further use by these Rebel marksmen. Volunteers were called for to perform this very dangerous duty.

The first to raise a hand was Sergeant Charles A. Hitchcock, Company G, 111th New York Infantry, who was quickly chosen for the task. A comrade who witnessed this unusual feat, wrote:

> He started on the doublequick, taking a zigzag course on beyond our skirmishers until he reached the barn. . . . With his bunch of papers he fired the barn in one corner, under which he found some hay. On his return he was wounded in the arm. . . . Upon reporting to General Hays the success of his mission, he handed the General a bunch of flowers picked up at the barn upon leaving it, these flowers, carefully preserved being now in possession of the Hays family.

In a letter written to his daughter just after the fight, Hays, himself, wrote about these flowers:

> The flower I sent to Grandma came from the garden [on] the field of Gettysburg, from the house where our pickets fought so wickedly, and which I afterward caused to be burned. It was given me by the Sergeant who volunteered to go forward amidst a shower of balls to burn the house. He fulfilled his mission and returned severely wounded.

Today, the site of the Bliss farm may be viewed by interested visitors to the Gettysburg National Military Park. Nothing remains of the buildings, however two small markers stand nearby which unfortunately indicate only a small part of the history which occurred there.

Truce

Between Cemetery Ridge and the William Bliss farm buildings an incident transpired which was uncommon during this particular battle. It was recorded in the memoirs of Lieutenant Tom Galwey, 8th Ohio Infantry, as occurring on July 3.

About thirty yards in front of my company stood a solitary tree which, I suppose, had been left as a shade for men in the harvest field. During the morning this tree became conspicuous on account of the well-aimed shots that came from it. We soon became aware that a couple of bold enemy sharpshooters had crawled up to it and were now practicing on any thoughtless man who offered himself as a mark.

About the middle of the forenoon a cry of, 'Don't fire, Yanks!' rang out, and we all got up to see what was coming. A man with his gun slung across his shoulder came out from the tree. Several of our fellows aimed at him but the others checked them, to see what would follow. The man had a canteen in his hand and, when he had come about half-way to us, we saw him (God bless him) kneel down and give a drink to one of our wounded who lay there beyond us. Of course, we cheered the Reb. . . . Whilst this was going on, we had all risen to our feet. The enemy too, having ceased to fire, were also standing. As soon as the sharpshooter had finished his generous work, he turned around and went back to the tree, and then at the top of his voice shouted, 'Down Yanks, we're going to fire.' And down we lay again.

The next day – the Fourth of July – a heap of Confederates was found under that tree. Whether the hero of the day before was one of the ghastly dead will probably never be known.

The "solitary tree" mentioned by Galwey was an old white oak which stood in that open field for probably one hundred and fifty years or more. As of June 20, 1987, it was the last still-living witness to the events portrayed by the lieutenant. However, on that date, this proud memorial of time and history was blown down in a severe wind storm.

Present-day site of the solitary oak tree (foreground) near the site of the Bliss farm (background).

The Flying Surgeon

The reader may remember a humorous incident recalled by Captain Thomas Livermore on a previous page. Here is another colorful episode which also was not forgotten by that same officer.

[On July 3] . . . about noon, I should think, finding myself at liberty to do so, I joined General [Winfield S.] Hancock and staff on the line of battle. . . . I recollect distinctly riding along from the 2d Division's rear to that of the 3d Division, [of the Second Corps] and while in rear of the latter, the crest on which its line was formed was so high as to conceal from us the rebel line; but just at this moment a large number, perhaps fifty, of our corps came rushing through the line to the rear in a great panic. They were our skirmishers, who had been driven in by the enemy. When General Hancock saw them running past his front, he turned about to his staff, who were following him, and in a tremendous rage cried, 'Go after them! Go after them!' Whereupon as one man, the whole of us started on a keen gallop after the fugitives, and by dint of hard words and sabers stopped their flight.

I shall never lose from the retina of my mind's eye the picture of Dr. Alexander Dougherty [medical director of the Second

Corps] at this juncture. The doctor was a very fat man, and the picture of good-nature. His uniform, which was never, or very seldom, renewed, did not serve to lengthen his short and broad figure, and he rode a very fat and sturdy black horse as phlegmatic and good-natured as he. The doctor, as may be inferred from his presence on this occasion, was not one of those members of the medical profession who so rigidly sheltered their bodies by the privilege of being non-combatants as never to visit the field in time of battle, but was noted for his frequent presence under fire, where he encountered danger rather with the equanimity of a philosopher than the martial spirit of the professed fighting man. Now, when the general turned about with the explosive command above quoted, the doctor did not deem himself a whit excused from the chase, and accordingly put spurs to his good-natured beast and, on the lumbering gallop, pursued the fugitives, his coat-tails flying, and his elbows out, as his horse rose with ponderous momentum to take a two-barred fence in front of him, that still is vivid before me and never fails to make me laugh.

Volunteer or Else!

In 1899, an officer of the 19th Massachusetts Infantry, John Adams, wrote of an incident he witnessed.

No matter how serious the battle, there is always a humorous side to it which an old soldier never loses. So it was at Gettysburg. When the fire was the hottest on the centre the battery that the 19th was supporting lost nearly all its men. The captain came to our regiment for volunteers to man the guns. Captain Mahoney was the first to hear the call. Going to Company E, he said, 'Volunteers are wanted to man the battery. Every man is to go of his own free will and accord. Come out here, John Dougherty, McGiveran and you Corrigan, and work those guns.'

Surgeon Taylor's Delicate Wound

Dr. William H. Taylor served in the Gettysburg Campaign with the 19th Virginia Infantry of Garnett's brigade. He was not shy about reporting this embarrassing personal experience.

"Our [aid] station on this field . . . [was] a little dell in a grove conveniently in the rear of the troops. Here we had a large collection of apple-butter pots, gathered from the surrounding country, which were filled with water to be used for the wounded."

[Taylor and his medical attendants felt secure and lazy until about one o'clock on July 3 when the great cannonade which preceded Pickett's famous charge commenced. By some miscalculation, his field hospital was at the very center and focus of the artillery fire.]

65

In a moment the air was filled with limbs of trees, scraps of butter-pots and yells of fleeing medical men . . . my horse, young and restive, had tangled himself in a tree. . . . I was thus for some minutes made an involuntary witness of the impressive spectacle. It is impossible to describe it. I question if in all civilized warfare there can be found anything more sublimely awful than the crash of a broad-side of cannon-shot through a stockade of apple-butter pots.

. . . Having at last released my horse I moved off. . . . I had gone only a little way when I suddenly felt what I have seen described in accounts of hangings as a dull thud. Dull as it was, it was sufficiently sharp to convince me . . . that I was slain; and I remember that I was much troubled in mind to know whether I had been honorably put to death by a legitimate missile, or had been ignominiously butchered by a butter-pot. . . . I hobbled vigorously away and [soon] . . . investigated my injuries. I found that there was nothing more serious than the loss of three or four cubic inches of tissue, which had been scooped out of me. . . .

With the pardonable vanity of a veteran who has been battered in the wars it has always been a delight for me to relate this incident. [In] years since, I taught science to the boys and girls of Richmond High School, where I at times relieved the aridity of scientific details with accounts of my military experiences, [where] I was accustomed to narrate this piteous story with much feelings. The girls especially would become deeply touched with sympathy for . . . their teacher . . . [and] would exclaim, 'Oh poor Doctor Taylor! Where were you wounded?' To this . . . I could only reply simply, 'At Gettysburg,' for to their untechnical minds it would have conveyed no information to tell them that it was in the gluteous maximus muscle!

Shellfire

During the two-hour Confederate artillery bombardment on the afternoon of July 3 preceding the attack known as "Pickett's Charge," the wounded Northern and Southern soldiers lying in the Christ Lutheran Church on Chambersburg Street in Gettysburg kept up a running dialogue with each other. One of those present, Thomas L. Hanna, 83rd New York Infantry, related this:

"[During the shelling] it goes without saying that the excitement in the church was intense. 'Give 'em hell!' faintly cried a dying reb. 'Feed it to them,' roared a Battery B man, and a hardened old sinner shouted, 'Look hyar, Yanks, you'uns had better say your pray-ers; if we'uns drap a shell in this er meetin' house you'uns won't know nuthin!'

"A yell, a cheer, and honors were even. . . . "

The Cowardly Color Bearer

Abner R. Small was a member of the 16th Maine Infantry and adjutant for the First Brigade, Second Division, First Army Corps at Gettysburg. He wrote in his memoirs of an incident which took place on Cemetery Hill at about two o'clock on July 3.

Colonel [Richard] Coulter, tearing up and down the line to work off his impatience, all of a sudden drew rein and shouted: 'Where in hell is my flag? Where do you suppose that cowardly son of a bitch has skedaddled to? Adjutant, you hunt him up and bring him to the front!'

Away I went, hunting for the missing flag and man and finding them nowhere; and returned in time to see the colonel snake the offender out from behind a stone wall, where he had lain down with the flag folded up to avoid attracting attention. Colonel Coulter shook out the folds, put the staff in the hands of the trembling man, and double quicked him to the front. A shell exploded close by, killing a horse, and sending a blinding shower of gravel and dirt broadcast. The colonel snatching up the flag again, planted the end of the staff where the shell had burst, and shouted:

'There Orderly; hold it! If I can't get you killed in ten minutes, by God, I'll post you right up among the batteries!'

Turning to ride away, he grinned broadly and yelled to me:

'The poor devil couldn't be safer. Two shells don't often hit the same place. If he obeys, he'll be all right and I'll know where my headquarters are.'

Recklessly he dashed down the line. In a few minutes he returned, with one arm dangling. I recall the expression of his pain-distorted face when I, in my anxiety, asked him if he would not dismount; it was almost one of reproof.

'No, no,' he said; 'not now. Who in hell would suppose a sharpshooter would hit a crazy-bone at that distance!'

The Dying Virginian

His duties completed, Lieutenant Small took time after the repulse of "Pickett's Charge" on the late afternoon of July 3 to aid the many Confederate wounded lying in a grove south of Cemetery Hill.

Near by I saw a handsome youngster; a Virginian, of Kemper's brigade, I think. I knelt beside him, and wondered if perhaps he was sleeping, he was so calm and still. He unclosed his eyes, and looked into mine with an intense questioning gaze, an appeal most beseeching, most eloquent; but I had no answer to the riddle. I asked him where he was wounded. He drew a hand slowly to his breast, and I knew there was little chance for him. I asked

67

him if he was afraid to die. He whispered, 'No, I'm glad I'm through.'

A spasm of pain closed his lids. I couldn't bear to leave him. I put my head down close to his and suddenly he opened his eyes again; and I shall never forget their unearthly beauty, nor the sweet, trusting look that spread over all his face as he said to me, with a motion as if he would throw his arms around my neck, 'I'm going home. Good-bye.'

I did weep; I couldn't help it. I don't remember his name; he may not have told it to me.

Little Brother

James A. Harwood, an officer in Company K, 53rd Virginia Infantry, was a participant in a most sad event on the hot afternoon of July 3, 1863. He explained:

When the [cannonade] ceased the shrill command of Pickett was heard 'Columns, forward, march,' and each brigade moved off. . . . We had not gone far, however, before the enemy's guns opened upon us and ploughed through our ranks, cutting down many a brave soldier. . . . The writer then being a Lieutenant was on the extreme left of the company, and having heard that Captain [James D.] Lipscomb was killed, [I] turned around and saw that brave soldier fall to rise no more.

Soon after Lieutenant Ferguson fell, as we supposed, mortally wounded, when rushing to the head of the company, the writer saw his little brother,* whom he had loved and sheltered in many a hard fought battle before, fall. Running up to him, the little fellow exclaimed: 'Brother James, go back to your company; I am not hurt much and you are now in command.' But it was not long ere this brave little soul, who was then shot through by two minnie balls, found a soldier's grave and went to the God he had so faithfully served.

Harwood, himself, was wounded a few minutes later while among the abandoned guns of Cushing's battery in the Union position at the Angle. A Yankee officer rode up and threw Harwood on the back of his horse and hurried him to the rear. When Harwood asked the Federal why he had been carried off so unceremoniously, he replied that he had captured a big Rebel officer and did not want him recaptured.

"Imagine his surprise and chagrin when I told him I was only a Lieutenant, and nearly a dead one at that!"

* Christopher E. Harwood

The Fighting Surgeon

A color bearer of the 1st South Carolina Cavalry, J. P. Malone, was wounded in the cavalry battle east of Gettysburg on July 3. He remembered his last sight before sinking into a state of insensibility from the injury.

> I would mention the conduct of Surgeon Joseph Yates as worthy of the highest admiration. Nor should the admiration be confined to his conduct on this occasion. Temperate, humane, untiring in his energy, unflogging in his zeal, he was still as brave as Julius Caesar. My last recollections of him on that ill-starred field place him at the head of the regiment, cheering it on with the most gallant bearing. Indeed this was the only objection that could be urged against him, and even then it was rather that he endangered his own life than that he neglected the lives of others.

Shortly afterwards, Surgeon Yates was *arrested* for his daring conduct in the cavalry fight at Gettysburg. A note within Malone's memoir stated:

> The rare occurrence of a man being arrested for fighting the enemy was presented after this battle. Surgeon Yates was soon released, however, on account of the circumstances of the case.

A Chinaman in the Ranks

A story much loved and repeated often by many battlefield guides at Gettysburg is that of a Chinese volunteer killed during the battle. A column in the local newspaper reported:

> Among the killed at Gettysburg was a young Chinaman known as John Tommy. He was attached to the first regiment Excelsior Brigade, Capt. Price's company in the engagements at Fredericksburg, Chancellorsville, and last at Gettysburg. John Tommy was one of the bravest soldiers in that bravest of brigades. . . . He seemed not to know what fear was, and was the universal favorite of all his fellow soldiers. He had not been wounded up to Gettysburg but on Friday's fight he was struck by a shell which tore off both legs at the thighs and he shortly bled to death.

He was actually John *Tomney,* a corporal who served with Company D, 70th New York Infantry.

General Meade's Advice

The commander of the Army of the Potomac, General George G. Meade, was known throughout the army for his sharp and often violent temper. A member of the 20th Connecticut Infantry, John Storrs, witnessed this characteristic in action on or about July 3.

> One man, or rather; I should say, one individual came to the commanding general, even while the battle was in progress, and with

a long story about his house having been used for a hospital, and complaining that they had buried several soldiers who had died of wounds in his garden, besides a large number of amputated limbs, thereby spoiling it. He wanted the general to give him a paper as a basis for a claim upon the government.

'Why you craven fool,' replied the indignant officer, 'Until this battle is decided you do not know, neither do I, if you will have a government to apply to, or if your property will not be confiscated by the conquerors. If I hear anymore from you I will give you a gun and send you to the front line to defend your rights.'

It seems hardly possible that within the limits of the brave old Keystone state, such descendants as these from men of the Revolution could have been found.

Tipsy Tippin

Although heavy use of alcohol in the armies was not an infrequent occurrence, it is somewhat unusual to find mention of higher-ranking officers being intoxicated while on duty, especially while in combat. One diarist, Private Lewis Schaeffer, 68th Pennsylvania Infantry, was not shy about recording the following:

> *Sat. July 4* We lay in front until 9 o'clock this morning when we were relieved. All is quiet at present. We captured near 3000 prisoners. Our colonel was put under arrest yesterday for being drunk. He left for Washington this morning where he was ordered to report himself.

In his official report of the battle, Colonel Andrew H. Tippin of that regiment stated that he was relieved of his command on July 3, with no reason given. He was replaced by Captain M. S. Davis. However, the regimental records *after* Gettysburg show Colonel Tippin still in command.

The Deadly Windmill

Jacob Hummelbaugh's farm sat along the Taneytown Road just in rear of the Union line of battle and east of where the Pennsylvania Memorial stands today. Due to the heavy fighting in and near that area, it soon became a temporary field hospital, used heavily by the Second Corps and run by Dr. Alfred T. Hamilton of the 148th Pennsylvania Infantry.

General William Barksdale of Mississippi was cared for here by the doctor and later died at the same location. At least one other death, a most unusual case, occurred here. Dr. Hamilton explained:

> The wounded were carried in during the night of the 3d in such numbers that they filled the barn floor and open space surrounding it. One poor fellow who was badly wounded seemed

to be in the way of those moving among the wounded and pained by being knocked about, got into the hopper of an old windmill after dark hoping to be undisturbed. A shell struck him and tore him to pieces as he lay coiled in the hopper. Strange to say I saw the same old mill many years afterward at the same barn, having been patched up and used.

Moonlit Apparition

Robert G. Carter of the 22nd Massachusetts Infantry took a short walk with a friend before midnight of July 3 to view the battlefield in front of his regiment's position on Little Round Top. Here is his description of the ground.

Our tour extended across the swale, inside our picket lines now occupied by the Pennsylvania Reserves. . . . The scenes of that spot . . . still linger on our memories. Masses of Kershaw's and Wofford's Brigades had been swept from the muzzles of the guns. . . . They were literally blown to atoms. Corpses strewed the ground at every step. Arms, heads, legs and parts of dismembered bodies were scattered all about, and sticking among the rocks and against the trunks of trees, hair, brains, entrails and shreds of human flesh still hung, a disgusting, sickening, heart-rending spectacle to our young minds. . . .

One man had as many as twenty canister or case shot through different parts of his body, though none through a vital organ, and he was still gasping and twitching. . . .

We retraced our steps. When nearly within our lines we witnessed a sight, or vision, rather, for often even now it rises before us like a phantom. The moon though slightly overcast, still threw its pale yellow, sickly light through the trees and among the rocks, bodies and wild weird surroundings of that blood-stained place. As we turned to go around a large rock, we suddenly came face to face upon a man, who seemed from his position to be partially reclining against a cedar tree. His cap was off – his hair thrown back, the moonlight showed a remarkably fine cut youthful face, which seemed turned upward to Heaven, as though in the act of prayer. It was an imploring, and yet a calm and resigned expression – his hands were clasped. We started back as though from an apparition, and for a full moment could scarcely believe that the figure was not alive, or else a marble statue shaded by the trees. He was dressed in the rebel gray, and it proved to be the body of a boy, firmly fixed in the forked branch of a small tree. He had caught as he fell, and growing suddenly rigid in death, had retained a life-like attitude. We were so startled that for a few moments we walked in silence.

Disillusionment and Desertion in the Confederate Army

In any war, many, if not most, combat soldiers soon become disillusioned. No matter what the cause; no matter how often manliness, duty, honor, and godliness – the essence of what is called "courage" – is called upon, there is no halting the inevitable. Once idealistic men suffer and face extreme hardship, disease, wounds, and death, many soon question every value and moralistic platitude placed upon them by the rest of civilization – the "civilization" of course, that is not doing the actual fighting.

So it was in the Gettysburg Campaign.

While the majority of the rank and file kept to their posts and did what was ordered or expected, many did not. Some, for one reason or another, had simply had enough. In this section we will examine examples of desertion by Confederates; Southerners, only, in this case because they were in the enemy's country as the invaders, and since it has been noted in researching many hundreds of sources that although it is not generally known, not all Rebel soldiers believed in their "cause."

In fact, I have found many recorded accounts, especially by North Carolinians, of disaffection, and outright hostility toward the Southern government. Many North Carolinians, some forced into the army, had no love for secession as felt by their neighbors in Virginia or South Carolina. It must be recalled that North Carolina was not a large slaveholding state, and it had a significant population of mountain dwellers who had always been known for their fierce independence. Many soldiers felt as this man, who, when asked, "How is it that we find North Carolina [wounded] almost everywhere?", answered: "The only reason we can give for it, is, that they try to wreak their vengeance upon us because our state was opposed to going out of the Union." Ironically, in the Battle of Gettysburg, while Virginia had fifty-eight infantry and cavalry regiments in action, and North Carolina had thirty-eight infantry and cavalry regiments in the fight, North Carolina suffered 1,350 combat deaths as opposed to Virginia's 837 deaths. Is it not a wonder that many of the "Old North State" questioned the secession movement and felt that they may be only cannon fodder?

Other examples include Mrs. Joseph Bayly, who lived just north of Gettysburg in 1863, who recalled:

> I . . . responded to a knock at the door about 2 o'clock in the morning [July 2] and found a woebegone little "Reb" about 17 years of age, who said he had been in the fight the day before; that he belonged to a North Carolina [unit]; that his regiment was broken up and scattered; that he had been wandering around all night keeping away from pickets . . . and he never intended doing any more fighting for the confederacy.
>
> He was given a suit of citizen's clothes and remained with the family until the battle was over. He is now living on a farm near the battlefield and the size of his family indicates that he has

been more successful in peaceful pursuits than those of war.

. . . [M]any of the [rebels] were loafing around [our] house . . . the second day indicated that there was a large number who were shirking their duty in keeping away from the danger line. Many of them never went back south with Lee's army, but went north while their defeated comrades went south.

The respected historian Bell I. Wiley agreed in part with this assessment. He wrote in 1943:

In the wake of Gettysburg the highways of Virginia were crowded daily with homeward-bound troops, [deserters] still in possession of full accouterments; and, according to one observer, these men 'when halted and asked for their furloughs or their authority to be absent from their commands, . . . just pat their guns defiantly and say *this is my furlough,* and even enrolling officers turn away as peaceably as possible.'

The Assistant Secretary of War [Confederate] estimated at this time that the number of soldiers evading service by devious means, but chiefly by unauthorized absence, reached 50,000 to 100,000.

Similarly, a Gettysburg newspaper reported the story of William Cranford,

. . . who deserted the Confederate army here, and was hidden by a farmer named Kuhns, in the Irishtown area. When the armies went south Cranford remained here, worked as a carpenter and eventually married a young lady from the New Chester area, Miss Mary Spangler, daughter of George and Ninetta (Wolf) Spangler.

Cranford, it seems, died as the result of an accident in 1890. He is buried in the Spangler section of a New Chester cemetery. The soldier left a wife and four children when he died, but Mary soon married an ex-Union soldier named James Frederick.

John Cunningham and family lived on a farm on the banks of Marsh Creek, just west of Gettysburg. After the battle, Mr. Cunningham's daughter remembered a boy who changed allegiances:

After [the rebels] were gone Father noted a mere stripling with his head down on the meadow gate crying as if his heart would break. When Father asked the cause of his grief, he sobbed out that 'Our men are gone and now the Yankees will kill me.' Father was a comforting person. He assured the boy that he wouldn't be killed, that there was food in Pennsylvania and it wasn't at all a bad place to be. Months later . . . he received a letter from this boy: 'Mr. Cunningham, what you told me about the Yankees is true – I'm in the Union army now.'

After watching Confederates march through her town on June 27, Rachael Cormany of Chambersburg, Pennsylvania, wrote in her diary:

> I pity some of the men for I am sure they would like to be out. At Dicksons they told me that 400 went at one time – gagged the guards and got off to the mountains and on to Harrisburg to help our men . . . J. [Jacob] Hoke told me this morning . . . that about 1000 had deserted.

After the campaign, it was very common to read reports of deserters in the Pennsylvania-Maryland area. Specifically, some residents of the Blue Ridge Summit, Pennsylvania area remembered a small community which was founded by Confederate deserters in a "cove" in the mountains nearby. This tight-knit settlement lasted well into the Twentieth Century.

Finally, it should be mentioned that in my research notes are *many* references to Rebels captured or wounded at Gettysburg who openly denounced the Confederacy and reported that they were drafted into the army and still held loyalties to the United States.

An example of this is the story of George L. Hadley, a conscript in the Southern army who was the son of John L. Hadley, a former Secretary of State of New Hampshire. Forced into the army while living in Georgia, Hadley was later wounded and captured during this battle. His father tried very hard to have him released from federal detention if he would take the oath of allegiance. George himself stated he would "take his own life, rather than leave the hospital a rebel prisoner." After giving his oath, Hadley was finally released. He remained a clerk in a field hospital for a while, and when his wound permitted, was sent home to New England.

PART V

The Retreat and Aftermath

The Overzealous Mr. Pierce

Saturday, July 4, 1863, was long remembered by the citizens of Gettysburg. It was the day they cautiously stepped out of their houses and found the Rebel army withdrawn from the town – soon to begin their retreat back to Virginia later that evening. Each person reacted in a different way.

James Pierce, who lived on Baltimore Street at the southwest corner of Breckenridge Street, was notified of the retreat by the Methodist minister. Pierce was so overjoyed that he immediately started on a run for Cemetery Hill to tell the Union troops the wonderful news. But a block from his house, he looked down and saw that he was still in his stocking feet. As he later said, "[I] thought to [myself]: 'No shoes! No hat! No coat! Why if I go out looking this way, they will certainly think I am demented!' "

Pierce turned to go back, and noticed a musket laying on the pavement. His daughter, Matilda, told what happened next.

> He picked it up, and just then spied a Rebel running toward the alley back of Mrs. Schriver's lot. Father ran after him as fast as he could and called: 'Halt!'
>
> The fellow then threw out his arms, and said: 'I am a deserter! I am a deserter!' To which father replied:
>
> 'Yes, a fine deserter you are! You have been the cause of many a poor Union soldier deserting this world; fall in here.' He obeyed; and as father was marching him toward the house he spied two more Confederates coming out of an adjoining building and compelled them to 'fall in.'
>
> These also claimed to be deserters; but the truth is they were left behind, when Lee's army retreated. He marched the three men out to the front street and as there were some Union soldiers just passing, handed his prisoners over for safe keeping.
>
> He then went into the house; put on his shoes and hat; took his gun and went up to the alley back of our lot. There he saw a Rebel with a gun in his hand, also trying to escape. Father called on him to halt. The fellow faced about, put his gun on the ground, rested his arms akimbo on it, and stood looking at him. Father raised his musket and commanded! 'Come forward, or I'll fire!'
>
> The Confederate immediately came forward and handed over his gun. On his way to the front street with his prisoner he captured two more and soon turned these over to our men.
>
> Father then examined his gun for the first time; and behold! it was empty.

Cut Down to Size

Lieutenant Benjamin F. Rittenhouse took command of Battery D, 5th United States Artillery when Lieutenant Charles Hazlett was mortally wounded on Little Round Top on July 2. Rittenhouse gave an account of unusual courage he witnessed on July 4.

> The day after the battle I rode to the Fifth Corps hospital, to see my wounded men. Beside a strapping big sergeant lay a little Irish bugler of Battery "I," Fifth Artillery, who had had both legs cut off pretty close up to his hip joint. The surgeons were probing for the ball in the sergeant's leg, and he was making considerable fuss. The little bugler grew impatient, and sung out, 'Stop your noise; what is the use of making such a devil of a

75

racket. I don't make any fuss, and I have been trimmed down, until I am not as long as a yard stick.'

Records show that Private Dennis Wallace was wounded in both legs and both were amputated at the thigh. He died on August 2, 1863, at Camp Letterman General Hospital, east of Gettysburg, and was buried on August 3 in Section 3, Grave 18 of the hospital cemetery. You may now visit his grave in the Soldiers' National Cemetery, U.S. Regulars section.

Bugler Wallace's gravesite in the National Cemetery.

Jugs

When the Confederate army was victorious on July 1 and held control of the town of Gettysburg for the following three days, everything seemed to be going well. Many Rebel soldiers had great fun taunting captive or wounded Union soldiers who were unlucky enough to be trapped inside the town which was now within Southern lines. Several Rebel officers who had been drinking stolen whiskey were especially cruel in their comments to these unfortunate Federal prisoners, some of whom could be found lounging about on the high front steps of the Christ Lutheran Church on Chambersburg Street.

On July 4 when the Confederates were pulling their stragglers together to join the retreat in progress, one wounded Yankee soldier on the church steps noticed a cocky Rebel he had seen the day before who had had two jugs of whiskey tied to each side of his saddle.

Jubilant over the defeat of the Southern army and seeing this now not-so-happy Rebel, he called out: *"Nary a jug today!"*

76

Twenty-four hours earlier he may have been shot for speaking so rashly.

General Lee's Pet

The well-known and respected Civil War historian, Burke Davis, gives the following anecdote in one of his many books which illustrates the tender side of Robert E. Lee, the great commander of the Army of Northern Virginia.

For months, at the height of the war, Lee had a pet hen which laid an egg under his cot each day – and he never forgot to leave the tent flap open for her. Lee saw to it that the hen traveled with the army, even on so fateful a campaign as the invasion which ended at Gettysburg. When he began the retreat from that field, and the hen was nowhere to be found, the commanding general joined the search for his pet, and was not content until she was discovered and safely perched in his headquarters wagon.

Later in the war, however, this chicken was finally killed and eaten.

The Color of Death

Sergeant John D. Bloodgood, a member of Company I, 141st Pennsylvania Infantry, recalled an interesting but gruesome phenomenon he witnessed on July 4.

I walked over a part of the battlefield and watched the burial parties at their work. One thing peculiar struck me, and that was the difference in appearance of the dead soldiers of the two armies. The rebel dead retained nearly their natural appearance, while our dead had almost invariably turned a very dark purple in the face. Why it was so I could not even guess. I came to the body of a Confederate soldier, and seeing a tin cup fastened to his haversack I unbuttoned it and kept it as a relic of the war. On the outside it was stained with his blood and bore the marks of hard service.

This is not the first time I have read of this peculiar and distinct discoloration of Union and Confederate dead. One other source speculated that it was due to the very different diets of the respective armies.

The Short Cut

Mary A. Horner, a resident of Gettysburg who lived on Chambersburg Street with her husband, Dr. Robert Horner, observed an unusual sight on Independence Day of 1863.

All day we were uneasy, and often alarmed; the enemy's guns were turned on us, and there were rumors that they would shell the town; the sharpshooters actively held us in subjection until dark . . . there were breastworks [thrown up] across Chambersburg Street. Some poor starved army horses that had been turned loose to pick up a living strayed up this street; walking, not in the middle, but in solemn procession, along the pavement. When they reached the breastworks, finding they could neither climb over nor go around, they turned aside into the hall of a dwelling whose door stood open. In single file they proceeded through this hall, the rooms on either side filled with wounded, to the porch which ran along the back building. This porch was slightly inclined, and in their weak condition several slipped and fell. The lady of the house, greatly unstrung by the terrible experiences of the preceding day, threw up her hands, exclaiming, 'Oh, Lord, what will come next!'

A Good Job

A day or so after the battle, Surgeon Alexander M. Parker and Hospital Steward E. T. Gatchell of the 1st Maine Cavalry, discovered four Confederate officers in an old building near Gettysburg. Each of these men had lost a limb from wounds received on July 3. The Rebel officers were soon removed to a Union field hospital where they were well cared for. Before leaving, however, one of the Confederates exclaimed:

"You'uns tried your best to see how many legs and arms you could shoot off. Well, you'uns did the job pretty well."

Tougher Than Necessary

A surgeon of the 26th North Carolina Infantry, Dr. William W. Gaither, narrated an incident on the Confederate retreat from Gettysburg which illustrates the toughness of some soldiers.

Dempsey Lancy and Robert Cruise, members of Company I, from Caldwell County, had been fighting off and on during the day. About evening R. C. says to D. L., 'Demps, I'll hurt you directly,' and proceeded to knock him down and pulled out his right eyeball. D. L. did not even report sick. Two days after, I found him lagging a little in the rear and asked him what was the matter. He said R. C. had pulled his eye out, but it was all right now.

What is even more astounding is that both of these men were suffering from malarial fever on this march when their personal fight broke out.

General Meade's Other Headquarters

Most readers familiar with the Battle of Gettysburg will have no difficulty naming the farmhouse which became famous for all time by its conversion into the headquarters of the Army of the Potomac. Any book dealing with the battle usually documents General George G. Meade's use of this small structure which was owned by Widow Lydia Leister and stood on the Taneytown Road.

However, what is not readily known, is that General Meade used *another* house as his headquarters from July 5 through 7, after the Leister farm became untenable when it was inundated by the wounded of both sides on July 3 and 4. The new headquarters site was the house of Peter Pfieffer which was situated on the east side of the Baltimore Turnpike several hundred yards southeast of the Evergreen Cemetery.

This circa 1820s building, which later served as a tollhouse, was the scene of much hectic and important activity, and was visited by many people, both civilian and military during those long summer days. This energy occurred as the mighty Army of the Potomac was being put into motion to hunt down and destroy Lee's retreating Confederate force after the Northern victory at Gettysburg.

Unfortunately, the old Pfieffer place is almost gone now. Although once an untouched jewel which had never felt the heavy hand of progress, it is now a tumble-down relic of its glory days – so far in disrepair that it would be impossible to save. The photograph presented offers a look into the past of the house when its front door still slammed and its floor boards creaked as generals and their staffs rushed to and fro on various military missions. Walls, doors, windows and floors cannot speak. But if they could, their moments would be limited as the old house slowly settles into the dust of time.

An 1863 view of Meade's other headquarters on the Baltimore Pike. (GNMP)

Western Pluck

This story was told about one of the Union First Corps' infantrymen left on the field after the retreat.

> . . . [A] soldier of the 'Iron Brigade' . . . had been wounded in the foot early the first day, in the vicinity of Willoughby's Run; and unable to walk when his regiment fell back, he crawled into the dense bushes which . . . fringed the banks of that little stream at many places. Here he remained from the forenoon of July 1st to the morning of the 5th when the retreat of Lee's army enabled ambulance details of the Unionists to visit this portion of the field . . .
>
> Through all these days our Westerner had kept quietly to his bush protection. When all was quiet around he would crawl down and lave his wound in the rivulet. When Confederates were passing he kept very still and, if they saw him at all they doubtless believed he was one of the many dead. He had a few hardtack about him, and these, from time to time, he ate, moistening them in the sluggish water of the stream.
>
> When found by the ambulance men he had taken off the lock of his gun and having thoroughly wiped and cleaned it, replaced it. Lee's rear guard was retreating very slowly. Early that morning the wounded man had seen some of them . . . watching for the Federal advance. He had somewhere gathered up two boxes of cartridges and these were beside him.
>
> When the soldiers in blue suddenly came upon him in his attitude of watchfulness and were about to lift him into an ambulance, his first words were, 'Hold on a minute, I thought I saw one of the Johnnies skulking around over there. I want to pop him over before I go.'

Free at Last

During the Confederate Army of Northern Virginia's invasion of Pennsylvania, some unfortunate free blacks were kidnapped and taken back with that army on its retreat to Virginia. However, on the other hand, a few of the many slaves who accompanied the Rebels were inadvertently left behind, or simply escaped. Here is an account of two of those slaves. Reverend George Duffield explained:

> The day before, [about July 5] near Dillstown [Dillsburg], on my way from Carlisle, while stopping at noon to bait our horses, away off in a far corner of the porch, sitting very quiet, and apparently very tired and hungry, I discovered two colored men, one of whom, especially, by the name of Harrison Ash, was a splendidly proportioned man, about six feet two inches in height, and who must have been a very valuable chattel to his

master, a Mississippi Colonel, when human flesh was at a premium like gold.

His story was as follows:

'I came here wid de Southern army, an' I've been wid it ever since de war begun. Friday we had a big fight, de biggest fight yit, an' we git an awful big lickin'. Friday night we had a 'treat. Me and Druro here was 'sleep under a tree. Rain poured down powerful, an' dey lef' us. So in de mornin', when we woke up, dey was done gone.'

'Why don't you follow them?'

'Followed dem long 'nuff; besides, dey trabbel too fast, an' we can't cotch up.'

'That is, you didn't want to follow them?'

'No, sah.'

'Wasn't your master kind to you?'

'Yes, mos' times; though de hardest lickin' he ever guv me was for what he did hisself.'

'You would rather stay in Pennsylvania, then?'

'Yes, sah; dey tell us dere in Mississippi, dat at the Norf dere's nuffin' but snow and ice all de year roun', but dis don't look much like it, I reckon, an' I'd as lief lib here as dar, I'm tinkin!'

'You've been thinking of a good many things to-day, I suspect, Harrison. Let me see that big hand of yours, and feel the grit of it. Who owned that hand yesterday?'

'Massa did.'

'He made it work for him. Who owns it to-day?'

'Reckon Harrison does hisself.'

'Stand up, Harrison; do you know it, – You are a free man, both by the laws of God and man. What work you do, you will be paid for; what pay you get, you can put in your own pocket instead of into your master's.'

Like one awaking from a dream, or like [a] man . . . long shackled and lying in a dungeon, just beginning to move his unfettered limbs to look upon the light of day, so was it with poor Harrison.

One wonders if somewhere in the Commonwealth of Pennsylvania a black family lives today – with the surname of Ash, and their ancestor was once a piece of property in Mississippi.

One Foot in the Grave

Teenager J. Howard Wert lived three miles south of Gettysburg on the Baltimore Pike near White Run. Filled with curiosity at so much to see, he visited many parts of the battlefield and many of the field hospitals. On one occasion he found himself on Culp's Hill where heavy fighting had taken place on July 2 and 3. Wert wrote:

An area of perhaps four acres was so thickly covered with the dead that it was scarcely possible to walk anywhere without treading on them. . . .

The burials were not completed till the 5th by which time the corpses had become so blackened and swollen that the spectacle was the most revolting that could be conceived. The dead here were more carefully interred than on almost any other portion of the field. Deep, wide trenches were made in which corpses were placed side by side and well covered. On an adjacent oak the burial parties would hew off the bark from one side and place in lead pencil the number buried in the trench; thus: '73 rebs buried to right,' '45 rebs in this trench,' etc., etc. There were seventeen of these trenches on a space not exceeding five or six acres. . . .

One . . . incident furnished by a member of the [147th Pennsylvania] regiment, is given to illustrate the horrors of this spot in July 1863, as well as the indifference produced by continued contact with the shocking scenes of war. Whilst details were burying the dead which had fallen in the attack on Culp's Hill, and one of the trenches was ready to cover, a member of one of the Ohio regiments in the brigade asked; 'How many are in this trench?' 'Seventy-three,' was the answer. 'Make it seventy-three and a foot' and suiting his actions to the word, he threw into the trench a foot, which had been torn from some rebel by a shell or shot.

Confederate burial trench in the Culp's Hill vicinity.

Water, Water, Everywhere . . .

Azor H. Nickerson, captain of Company I, 8th Ohio Infantry was wounded on July 3 following "Pickett's Charge" as the Confederates shelled the Union lines in an effort to allow many of their soldiers to escape capture, and prevent a counterattack by Federal forces. Nickerson's wounds were severe; one missile through an arm, the other through his lungs.

On July 4 the captain was taken to the crude field hospital of the Second Corps, where among other terrible discomforts he had to lie outside in a pouring rain. Nickerson had a vivid and indelible memory of that time:

> . . . [T]oward morning [of July 5] I was seized with an awful thirst. Though the rain was pouring down my face and over my now totally unprotected body, I wanted water as I had never before wanted it. I called, and called again and again, but no one came. . . . Finally a sergeant of my regiment [Philip Tracy], who was lying near, answered and said that he would try and get some water for me. I heard him get up and the rattling of his canteen, as he started down to the creek for the coveted drink, but he did not return. He had been badly wounded himself, and daylight showed that in his effort to succor his fellow-soldier, he had fallen near the banks of the stream and there bled to death.
>
> The hope that had been raised and disappointed seemed to make me more thirsty than ever. A stream of water was boiling, bubbling, and running within my hearing; my face and body were drenched; and yet it seemed as though I should die of thirst.
>
> Since then I have been on the deserts of Arizona when the mercury would have registered not less than a hundred and ten in the shade – had there been any such luxury – and no one knows how much higher "in the open;" not a drop of water within a distance of forty miles; and so thirsty that my tongue was swollen till I could not speak; and yet the thirst endured on that July night at Gettysburg lives in my memory as exceeding in intensity that of all other occasions.

Captain Nickerson lived to rise to the rank of major, and served with the postwar army fighting Apaches in the Southwest.

Altercation at Mrs. Wade's

Almost anyone familiar with the story of the Battle of Gettysburg has certainly heard of the accidental death of Mary Virginia Wade, a little past eight o'clock on the morning of July 3, 1863. "Jennie" was in the act of mixing dough in the kitchen of her sister's house on Baltimore Street when she was struck and killed by a bullet probably fired by a Confederate soldier in the John Rupp tannery office building nearby.* What may not be widely known is what occurred at the unfortunate girl's mother's home two days later.

On the evening of July 5, just twenty-four hours after her daughter was buried in the graveyard of the German Reformed Church, Mrs. Mary A. Wade entertained a visitor, Reverend Alexander, in her house on Breckenridge Street. Another person in the house at that time was Major Michael W. Burns, 73rd New York Infantry, who had commanded his regiment during the battle. It is quite likely that Alexander was at Mary Wade's to help comfort her during her time of grieving, but it is a mystery as to why Burns was there and not with his regiment. We may never know why the following happened, but there is no doubt some sort of altercation took place. Presented here are the military court's charges and specifications against Major Burns:

Charge 1st – Conduct prejudiced to the character of the army.

Charge 2nd – Conduct unbecoming an Officer and Gentleman.

> In this: the said Michael Burns, did upon [S]unday evening July 5 enter the house of Mrs. Wade, a resident of the City of Gettysburg while grossly intoxicated; and did in the presence of the family of said Mrs. Wade commit a violent assault on Rev. Walter S. Alexander, Delegate of the U.S. Christian Commission for the State of Maryland, presented at his head a pistol and threatening to blow out his brains, and striking him with his sword cut him on the head and inflicted a serious wound.

No more is known of the incident. Burns must have been a rowdy fellow, however. Born in Ireland in 1834, he served during the entire Civil War, and was mustered out as Lieutenant Colonel of the 73rd New York Infantry in June of 1865. During his military career he was brought up on charges *three times,* but was never cashiered. (My thanks to Ed Raus for this good source.)

The old house where this all happened can yet be seen at 51 Breckenridge Street in Gettysburg.

*Incidentally, when first reported in a Gettysburg newspaper right after the battle, it was said that a "Union" sharpshooter had accidently killed Jennie.

Mrs. Hanness's Long Search

The following story was told by J. Howard Wert in 1907:

> In a happy home of Central New York lived a family of three when the dark war cloud burst on our land, a loving husband, a devoted wife and a son of seventeen, a brave and noble lad – the only fruit of their union.
>
> Father and son joined the same company of a New York regiment. Both fell at Gettysburg.
>
> Amongst the earliest arrivals on that field of death was the

stricken mother. With difficulty she obtained from the Harrisburg provo-marshal a permit to continue her journey. She walked ten miles through the mud from New Oxford to Gettysburg and found a home in the house of that noble man, David Warren, of Carlisle street, whose latch-string was ever out, through this whole period of calamity, to those who searched for their loved ones.

Her husband mortally wounded had been carried into a private house and had already breathed his last. Her son could nowhere be found. She searched over miles and miles of hospitals, in fields and barns, in churches and warehouses. She enlisted hundreds in the quest.

Then, with a lifelong grief in that gentle heart, she turned to the suffering crowd around her and went to the Second corps field hospital where thousands moaned as they hovered between life and death. Daily as a volunteer nurse she passed from cot to cot, prayed with the dying, soothed the anguish of the living; yet all the time hoping against hope that, in some mysterious way, she would find that lost son.

Mrs. Hanness never did find her son. Young De Grasse Hanness had been killed on July 1 and was evidently buried in an unmarked grave. Her husband Elias, aged forty-three, was wounded on July 1; he died on the 15th and was first buried in the Presbyterian graveyard in Gettysburg, but is now interred in the Soldiers' National Cemetery. Both father and son served in Company C, 147th New York Infantry.

J. Howard Wert personally knew Mrs. Hanness. After her daily work at the hospitals was completed she would often visit the home of his parents, Catherine and Adam Wert, who lived on the Baltimore Turnpike. Wert described her as a woman with a pleasant face, auburn hair and clear blue eyes, who, despite the sadness she carried, always had a cheerful word and a subdued smile for all.

Not Out of Range

Elizabeth "Sallie" Myers, a schoolteacher and resident of Gettysburg, nursed many wounded men both in the Catholic Church and in her own home during and after the battle. While caring for these men she heard this tale:

One of the soldiers in our house had lost a leg. My two youngest sisters often sang for him, and he would tell them stories of his experiences. I remember he said [that] in [the] battle the troops were exposed to such a storm of bullets that the colonel ordered them to lie down. So down they lay, all except the colonel, who was very short and fat. Some of them shouted for him to lie down also, but he responded: 'Why should I lie down? I'm as tall then as when I'm standing up.'

The Awful Noise of Battle

While walking over the battlefield in the present day, one may still find certain areas which are relatively free from noise pollution. Granted, planes and helicopters fly over regularly; cars, motorcycles, mopeds, and especially buses add to the sometimes terrific din. But in a few areas, especially when the summer months are over, the National Military Park can be a peaceful and even serene haven on this noisy planet.

That is why most visitors to the historical field are unable to comprehend just how loud the sounds are that a battle generates. This idea unexpectedly occurred to me once again while reading what Henry Meyer, 148th Pennsylvania Infantry, had noticed just after the three days of fighting ended:

> Citizen visitors in flocks came to see the field and Army. A number asked me why the soldiers talked so very loud to each other; so fierce, when they seemed not angry. I said we are all hard of hearing, nearly deaf, from the awful noise of battle.

So there it was. Noise! Most of us forget to include that sensation when thinking or reading or listening to stories of the great clash of armies at Gettysburg.

Soldiers were not the only creatures affected by this phenomenon. Birds and animals were frightened terribly by the muskets, cannon fire, and the voices of over 160,000 men engaged in the fury of combat. Most of the poor animals could not escape far, but the birds were another matter. There is ample proof to verify that most of the feathered population took wing for happier regions, as noted in the next few comments.

Sophronia E. Bucklin, a volunteer nurse, in describing her visit to Culp's Hill several weeks after the fight said:

> Amid all our buoyancy and interest in the things around us, at times the sigh of the wind grew unspeakably sad, as though ghosts haunted it, and burdened it with woe. No birds sang to us from the depths of the dismantling woods. . . .

Dr. Henry Baugher, Pennsylvania College president and professor, remarked after the battle in a sermon that "for one entire month, no note of a bird was heard in the campus where they were otherwise in abundance. The cannonade had frightened them away."

Mary Horner of Gettysburg spoke afterwards of the horrible plague of flies that descended upon the town and battlefield. She also remarked, "Even the birds of the air were awed into silence by the terrible tragedy; for it is a curious fact that not a song of a bird met our ears for weeks after the battle."

Reverend George Duffield of the Christian Commission recalled:

> Whether it was owing to the noise, the smoke, the universal presence of the soldiers, or the noisome and pestilential atmos-

phere, I do not know, but certain it is, that the orioles, robins, and other birds, so plentiful about the cemetery before the battle, had entirely disappeared from it. Singularly enough, the very first, and indeed the only bird I saw on the battle-field was a solitary turtle-dove, sitting in perfect silence. . . .

A bank clerk who lived on York Street, T. Duncan Carson, made some interesting remarks about a certain species of bird. He said:

You might think the buzzards would have swarmed to the battlefield, and we used to have a popular guide here who declared that they gathered from the four corners of the earth to prey on the dead. He described how when they rose from their horrid feast, they darkened the sky.

[You may ask] why he told such a yarn as that . . . well, it amuses people. They want things made exciting.

Really there were no buzzards here, probably because they were frightened away by the smell of the powder and the noise of the cannonading. They never made their appearance till several months later.

However, a black field hand "Isaac" who lived and worked on a farm four miles from Gettysburg remembered:

I guess we must have been saved from a pestilence by the buzzards. There were multitudes of them. . . . At night they would go to the woods and roost and you couldn't walk through under the trees they were so thick. It wouldn't have been pleasant, for they were throwing up and everything else.

Photograph of a Dead Man

One of the most famous war photographs of all times is the Timothy O'Sullivan image of a dead Confederate soldier behind a stone breastworks position at Devil's Den. For many years the photo was labeled as a "dead sharpshooter" killed while engaged in picking off Union soldiers defending Little Round Top. Several years ago in a prominent national magazine, the Southerner was even claimed to have been identified as a Virginia soldier.

In 1975, William A. Frassanito wrote his now famous book, *Gettysburg – A Journey in Time.* In this study of Gettysburg battlefield photographs, Frassanito explains how the body seen in the photo was that of an ordinary soldier who was killed about forty yards west of the breastworks position and who had been moved by the cameramen into the Devil's Den area as a prop to add realism to the scene. Frassanito identified the corpse as possibly that of a member of the 1st Texas or 17th Georgia. The man could not have been a Virginian as there were no units from that state engaged in the Devil's Den area.

There is no doubt that through the last 100 plus years, many people have wondered who this young soldier might have been. Killed in the prime of his life, he has remained an elusive shadow of a man, his image haunting our minds and that battlefield scene forever more.

However, just this year I was speaking to a friend, Edward Guy, who is a guide on the battlefield. Ed is not only one of the most knowledgeable students of the battle, but he is also kind and helpful to a fault. One day in the library of the Gettysburg National Military Park, he told me he thought he had identified the mysterious Confederate in that well-known photograph. Ed believes he is Private William L. Langley, Company E, 1st Texas Infantry, who was killed on July 2 in the attack on Devil's Den while a member of Robertson's brigade, Hood's division.

Sure enough, after examining a picture of Langley in a book on Hood's division, he had me convinced. The two soldiers looked identical. Anyone viewing good copies of these photographs would be hard-pressed to disagree. Of course, there is no guarantee that Ed is correct, but one must acknowledge that he may have come the closest ever to unravel a long-standing mystery of the Civil War.

Dead Confederate soldier at Devil's Den.

Papa's Boy

While on the march trailing the Confederates during the retreat from Gettysburg, Thomas J. Livermore, who was in command of the ambulance train of the Union Second Corps, stated in his memoirs:

[On July 7] I heard a laughable incident. . . . When General French commanded the 3rd Division of our corps he had a son on his staff as aide who was rather an effeminate youth, and this son went with a message from the general to Colonel [Samuel S.] Carroll, commander of the 1st Brigade, who was a very brusque soldier. He said to Colonel Carroll: 'Pa desires you to do so and so;' to which Colonel Carroll replied, 'Who in hell is *your pa?*'

The Spring Forge Scavengers

J. Howard Wert, a lad of about seventeen in 1863, lived with his mother and father Adam and Catherine Wert about three miles south of Gettysburg. Many years after the battle he still remembered a few of the unsavory characters who descended like vultures onto the recent field of strife.

The battle of Gettysburg and its hospital period gave opportunity for manifestations of the most unbounded loyalty, charity and helpfulness. It was seamed with streakings of innate selfishness, depravity and ruthless disregard of humanity that surge to the surface in every great catyclysm [sic]. One of the very meanest of these exhibitions was given by the thieves and plunderers who fattened over the ground before the dead were all buried, and who continued their ravages for weeks.

They came in teams to load up their loot. They traveled day and night to hasten to the raven's feast. Spring Grove, then called Spring Forge, was not, in 1863, the beautiful and prosperous town . . . [it is now].

There was, however, a small paper mill located in it; and there were through that section a number of nondescript scavengers, of mixed nationalities, who made a living by scourging the country over and collecting rags which were sold to the mill.

These men, with their teams drawn by spavined and disreputable specimens of horseflesh, hastened to Gettysburg, ostensibly to collect the clothing profusely scattered over the field of slaughter and in the environs of the hospitals. But all was fish that came to their net – guns and sabres on the battle ground, supplies for the wounded left unguarded after they had been unloaded, the few remaining chickens of devastated farms, the pigs that had scampered in terror from their shot-torn stys [sic] to the woodland and had not been reclaimed. They pilfered from the living and robbed the bodies of the dead. They even resurrected corpses from their shallow entombment in the hope that some valuable might be found on the festering body.

At points a little more remote from the heaviest conflict, where some fragments of fencing were yet standing, they made short cuts by throwing down what yet remained as they drove around in their career of plunder, and thus it was that three of the boldest met their finish.

As the caravan was about to start York county way, loaded with its miscellaneous loot, a farmer's wife expostulated with them about their wanton destruction of what little was left. They cursed her in mongrel English and 'Pennsylvania Dutch.' Her son, who came up, not feeling competent to fight at close quarters three stalwart men, took a surer and more effective means of revenge. He knew where there was a squad of Captain Smith's* men at a short distance and to them he hied.

Fifteen minutes later the cavalrymen swooped down on the marauders. Cursing didn't go; neither did entreaties. Prayers, tears, profanity and 'Pennsylvania Dutch' were all wasted articles when it came to dealing with Captain Willard Smith's 'Forty Thieves.'

The dose the rag gatherers received was an ample sufficiency to give them the shivers from all future life at the barest glimpse of a blue uniform. Their plunder was confiscated; their teams and they themselves put to work. The work they did was hard work; it was menial and repulsive work, but there were glittering bayonets to enforce activity and diligence in their tasks. It was a long time before the trio ever saw Spring Forge.

When they did they were sadder men; likewise, wiser. They had lost all desire for battlefield plunder.

*Captain Smith and his men were part of a provost marshal's detachment left behind to gather and guard government property left on the battlefield.

Fearful Expectations

This pathetic scene was acted out in one of the field hospitals which were scattered in all direction in and around Gettysburg. It was indelibly imprinted in the memory of John Foster, a Philadelphia civilian who did good service among the wounded.

In one of our rambles over the field we found a soldier who, although not apparently a severe sufferer, was anxious to [speak to a doctor]. The surgeon of our party, after some cursory examination of his wounds, remarked,

'You must have that limb examined, my good fellow; I will send for you tomorrow and have you brought up.'

A look of unutterable longing came into the soldier's face. He knew the thought of the surgeon's mind; the examination meant amputation, and he exclaimed, half-savagely, but with a childish entreaty mellowing the defiance of his voice,

'I can't lose that leg – I can't, I can't!'

'But, why?' we said.

He paused a moment, and a startled look passed over his face, as if in a flash he had thought of his dear ones at home and their dependence upon him, and his possible inability to care for them in the future. Then he answered haltingly,

'Because; because, Sir, I have use for it.'

Lydia Smith – Heroine

J. Howard Wert left behind an account of a totally different kind of hero than the usual stories portray.

But I promised . . . to speak . . . of Mrs. Smith. . . . She belonged to a despised and down-trodden race, for she was a colored woman. She was poor, yet she had a little money saved up, a trifle at a time, by years of labor. Her name was Lydia Smith. . . .

From a white neighbor she hired a ramshackle wagon with which she did hauling, and a horse. The horse was a pile of bones, else probably he would not have been in Adams County at all but mounted by a Confederate cavalryman.

Lydia circled widely through the farm section around Bendersville and York Springs, which had not been so utterly devastated as the region contiguous to Gettysburg. Eloquently she told of tens of thousands of suffering men:

'I thank de good Lawd that put it into my heart to try to do something for these poor creatures.'

When she could get donations of delicacies and suitable clothing, she accepted them. When donations failed, she bought till she had spent the very last penny of her little hoard acquired by years of frugality and toil.

But now the wagon was heaped high to its full capacity, and she turned toward the hospitals miles away. The old horse swayed and tottered, but Lydia walked by his side and led him on over dusty highways and rugged hills till, at length, the tents were at hand.

And then Lydia, feeling not the weariness from many miles of travel, began to distribute the articles she had brought – to Union soldiers, of course?

No! Union and Confederate lay side by side; and that noble colored woman saw not in the latter the warriors who were striving to perpetuate the slavery of her race. She saw only suffering humanity; and to Union and Confederate alike was impartially given the food, the clothing, the delicacies that had been obtained by the expenditure of her last penny.

The Saga of "Big Tom" Norwood

On July 10, 1863, General Robert E. Lee sent General James E. B. Stuart a confidential dispatch, written from a bivouac of the Rebel army near Hagerstown, Maryland. The dispatch mentioned a wounded North Carolina lieutenant who had just arrived at headquarters with information concerning the Yankee army. The young officer had recently escaped from a field hospital near Gettysburg.

Historian E. B. Coddington wondered about this officer, and what exciting drama led him to Lee's breakfast table seven days after the great battle. Coddington, in 1963, through some luck and good research, uncovered the following:

> . . . Thomas Lenoir Norwood was born in Lenoir, North Carolina in 1845. At the age of sixteen he entered the University of North Carolina, where he proved to be a brilliant student gifted with a rare combination of intelligence, courage, wit, musical talent and charm. He was known affectionately as 'Big Tom.' . . . In 1862 . . . he entered the Confederate army as private and in the next few months worked himself to first lieutenant.

Mr. Coddington later discovered a letter written by Tom's cousin, Sarah Tillinghast, about his Gettysburg adventures. It read:

> I cannot refrain from telling you all about Tom's adventures. He got thro' the first days fight without injury and was making a desperate charge upon those breast works when he was shot thro' the left shoulder the ball passing in such a way as not to injure a bone or leader. He tried to retreat but fainted from loss of blood and being very near the works, the first thing he knew the Yankees had him over in their rear[.] [W]hen he had recovered sufficiently to walk they took him three miles back, where he laid two days & nights on the ground in the rain with only his pants & a ragged shirt on, having lost his blanket in the charge & his coat being ruined by the blood.
>
> After the retreat of our army they were put into a college at Gettysburg, and seeing no guard he determined to make his escape. They were very kindly treated by the enemy but as there were so many and every comfort was divided by long division so that the prospect was a bad one. [Legend has it that Norwood put on an academic gown to make his escape.] He walked off on the Chambersburg road (the way the army came) about two hours by sun & went on unmolested till nine o'clock, having reached the top of

the South mountain, where a man came upon him from a by path enquiring who he was & where he was going, he tried to bluff him off but he would not be bluffed off & finally asked him if he was a Rebel, whereupon he confessed, and this man said well then you have found a friend, 'come home with me & I will help you' – he took him about four miles thro' torrents, over rocks etc. in the pitch dark until about midnight they arrived at the place. The old lady gave him a good supper & they dressed him up in a suit of laborers clothes but as the man was somewhat smaller than Tom they were not very becoming.

He started the next morning & after wandering over 'rocks & dens & the caves of the earth' [Tom] fell into the road our army had taken when they retreated – he went on falling in constantly with Yankee soldiers, walking & talking freely with them, without being suspected, about two hours by sun he came into Waynesboro about 12 miles from Hagerstown on the Chambersburg road – here he stumbled on the whole Yankee army and just as he was beginning to think the thing done, he was hailed by an old man who took him for a harvest hand looking for work, the old man wanted him to go on toward the rebel lines and help him get in his crop, he agreed and Tom gave his name as John Knouse. 'Oh, yes, said the old man I know your folks well!,' he being well known easily got Tom a pass & he went with the old man before a Brig. Gen. and got it signed, when once through the pickets he gave the old fellow a slip & made for our lines – Our pickets sent him to Gen. Johnson, com.[manding] post, he sent him to Gen. Ewell & he again to Gen. Lee. He arrived at his headquarters about midnight having walked 40 miles that day.

Next morning he went to see the General: was treated very politely, complimented on his adventures, gave a good deal of information, and finally invited to breakfast, sat by the General in his uncouth garments feeling as large as you please. He then reported to his Colonel & was sent to Richmond with the wounded & is now at Uncle Williams, he says he is in robust health & suffering very little from his wound, will get a furlough if he can.

Tom survived the war despite the fact that he received five wounds between 1862 and 1865. He became a teacher and worked at schools in Tennessee, Mississippi, and Texas, but died suddenly in 1888.

Bones

During the Battle of Gettysburg there were literally thousands of horses and mules killed and injured, some hurt beyond the help of medical aid. Following the three days of fighting, several hundred of these wounded animals were gathered and led to a field near Rock Creek across from the present National Military Park road which runs near Spangler's Spring. This spring was south of Culp's Hill and east of the Abraham Spangler farm along the Baltimore Pike, and became well-known during the battle. The animals were shot, and for many years the bones of these horses lay in a thicket on the north side of a little run which flows down into Rock Creek.

Today, the bones and thicket are long gone, but the site which beheld the last moments of these four-legged Gettysburg veterans can today still be viewed by the present day visitor.

A "Dear John" Letter

Mrs. C. A. Elher of Lancaster, Pennsylvania, was one of the many volunteer nurses who came to Gettysburg after the battle to care for some of the 21,000 wounded left behind by the two armies. One of her reminiscences concerned an Englishman, a color bearer of a New York regiment, who she found lying wounded in the Christ Lutheran Church.

In wishing to help the young man, Mrs. Elher asked what she could do for him. He told her that "there was one on whom all his hopes centered, who made life precious and desirable to him," and he wished for Mrs. Elher to write a letter to this woman.

Nurse Elher said:

> To her I wrote a letter, telling of his sad state, how he had fallen, bleeding and wounded; and, at his request, added, that though he had lost his leg, he was proud to tell her he had saved the regimental colors, and his own life, too, was still spared him, which was only made valuable by thoughts of her.

Each day thereafter Mrs. Elher asked the soldier if he had received a reply.

> [And] . . . I discovered his great anxiety at not receiving an answer to his letter. I begged him to be patient, and explained that the mail had been interrupted . . . all of which failed to reassure him; and when, going to him the next morning, I saw lying beside him on his pillow a letter, directed by a lady's delicate hand, I felt all would be well. Yes, the letter was delicately directed, delicately written, and delicately worded – but its meaning was not to be misunderstood. It was a cool, calm regret that she could no longer be his; to which was added the fear that the loss of his limb might affect his prospects in life. He handed me the letter to read, with a look of fixed despair – buried his head in the pillow, and wept like a child. To him she had been the embodiment of all that was true and lovely; and while others had mothers, sisters and friends, she was his all. The blow had been sudden, but sure. When he looked up again, his face bore the pallor of marble, and I saw there was no hope . . . he lingered two days [then] he died, and his last words were 'tell her I forgive her.'

The Prodigal Cow

Albertus McCreary, the young Gettysburg civilian whom we have already met told another of his battle experiences:

> We had an old cow that had been in the family for years, and the morning of the first day of the fight we put her in pasture as usual. This pasture was near the edge of town. Of course, we saw nothing of her during the three days of fighting. Often one of us would say, 'I wonder what has become of the old cow.' The general opinion was that we had seen the last of her. On the morning of the fourth day, Father, my brother, and I took a walk over the field to see if we could find any trace of her. We saw many terrible sights. Dead soldiers were lying around thick, dead horses, and cow skins and heads; from this last we soon came to the conclusion that our cow had been killed for food like the rest, so we gave her up.

> As we were eating supper one evening a week or more after the battle, we heard a familiar bellowing in the street. Everybody sprang from the table and rushed out. There stood our dear old cow, looking as happy as it is possible for a cow to look at being home again. We petted and hugged her in our pleasure at finding her alive, and soon had her in the stable in her own familiar stall. Then we discovered that she had a bullet-hole in her neck and in her side. She was not severely hurt, however, and both bullets came out eventually. We found out later that all the cows in that particular field had gotten out in some way . . . and had wandered off about ten miles from town, beyond the firing-line. After the battle they all found their way back to town.

The Little Soldier

It is hard for people in the Twentieth Century to believe that in a war as terrible as the Civil War, where over 660,000 men died both in combat and due to various diseases, that some soldiers actually took their children to war to share the dangers of battlefield and camp life. Here is an example of that very fact of life in the Nineteenth Century.

Mrs. Emily B. T. Souder, who served as a volunteer nurse for many weeks at Gettysburg after the battle, wrote the following in a letter to a friend in Philadelphia:

> A Captain in an Ohio regiment died yesterday directly opposite to the house where we were staying, [on Baltimore Street just north of the corner of Breckenridge Street], another wounded man lying on the floor in the same room, and the Captain's wife in spasms all day. It was pitiful to witness the efforts at consolation made by her son, a little fellow in uniform, who had been with his father in the army, although a mere child.

95

The officer was probably Captain John Costin, Company F, 82nd Ohio Infantry, who was wounded on July 1 and died on July 11.

Dooley's Story

About the tenth of July, wounded Confederate Lieutenant John Dooley, 1st Virginia Infantry, was convalescing at the Second Corps hospital on the Jacob Schwartz farm about three miles south of Gettysburg. He wrote in his diary of an incident which showed that at least a few surgeons had some notion of how deadly an infection could be. (Remember, Joseph Lister's revolutionary pronouncements on aseptic surgery were still several years in the future.)

> The Yankee surgeon in charge of all the wounds in these parts is a *Georgian!* But being educated at [West] Point he has thought it incumbent on him to deny his native land and join with its enemies. He is a very fine looking man and had his hand in a sling, for yesterday when operating upon a gangrened wound, the knife with which he was operating cut his finger slightly; and he very sensibly . . . had his finger immediately amputated.

I attempted to identify this surgeon, and fortunately had some success. Only one Georgian-born, U.S.M.A. graduate at Gettysburg fit the description. He was Medical Inspector John M. Cuyler who worked on the wounded from July 10 – 25.

Heads Up

While on the retreat from Gettysburg, Lieutenant Randolph H. McKim, an aide de camp to General G. H. Steuart, was required to halt for a time with the Southern army at a small town in Maryland. He said:

> At Williamsport the following amusing incident occurred. While the wagon-trains were massed there waiting for the river to fall, the enemy's cavalry approached and shelled the banks of the river. There is a deep hollow or depression there on the north side of the Potomac, and here the wagons were parked. A Confederate quartermaster officer approached the spot during the artillery fire and was amazed to observe that not a single teamster was to be seen. He could not account for it, until he happened to look toward the river, and there saw hundreds of black heads just showing above the water. The negro teamsters with one accord had plunged into the river to escape the shells, and were submerged to the neck!

To Each His Own

The volunteer nurse, Mrs. C. A. Elher, who travelled with a patriotic group from Philadelphia to assist the wounded after the battle wrote of an interesting character she met while working in a First Corps hospital located in the Christ Lutheran Church on Chambersburg Street.

There was an old Netherlander . . . with three shocking wounds, who seemed to think them nothing compared to the damage done by the battle to his favorite cap. As soon as he was able, it was nicely brushed, and he commenced decorating it. Every little bright bit of ribbon or button that he could get was sewed on until it looked like a mosaic work, and at every addition he would set it on the window and admire it for hours; and when the Government supplied the hospitals with fly-nets, instead of putting his to its legitimate purpose, Peter hung his cap on a nail and covered it with his net, much to the amusement of the whole hospital.

The Wild Texan

Colonel Robert Powell of the 5th Texas Infantry had been wounded and captured in the attack on the Union position at Little Round Top. As he lay with some of his men in a field hospital tent in the rear of the Federal lines he noted this incident:

There were eighteen of us in an open tent. Just outside and under what is called an individual tent was self-quartered a peculiar specimen known as a wild Texan, who occupied himself looking after and nursing [his] fourteen wounds.

Among our first visitors was the Governor of Pennsylvania, who looked as if he had been roughing it with his militia. His companions were new and fresh all over, painfully and embarrassing[ly] new.

One of the party approached the human fragment under the little strip of canvas and asked: 'What can I do for you, my good fellow?'

'Well, mister,' [the wild Texan] replied, 'now you don't think I am good and I am not a feller. We uns didn't come among you uns to ask favors, and I reckon I will just remember the fourteen I got and not be obligating myself to you for anything better.'

That man finally escaped and reached the 'Land of Dixie.'

Deadshot

It is a rare occurrence when a soldier admits to the killing of another human being; even in the context of war when his country has effectively legalized murder. An exception to that general observation is found in a letter written by Corporal Eugene B. Kelleran, Company I, 20th Maine Infantry, to his brother shortly after the Battle of Gettysburg. Kelleran was a twenty-six-year-old farmer from Cushing, Maine, who participated on July 2 in the defense of Little Round Top as a member of Vincent's Third Brigade of the Fifth Army Corps. The following is an excerpt from that letter. My thanks to Glen Hayes of Pleasantville, New York, for permission to publish it, with all of its misspellings.

Near Williamsport, Maryland
Sunday, July 12, 1863

Dear Brother,
   I take this opportunity to let you know that I am well[.] I hope this will find you all the same. When the rebs left Gettysburg we followed & most evry day we have a skirmish with them[.] day before yesterday Co. E was skirmishing & had 7 men taken prisoners & Sargeant [Gordiner] S[ch]wartz shot of Waldoborough, & another man severely wounded in the side[.] I helped to carry him to the rear. yesterday we was skirmishing but none of [the company] was hurt by the balls come very close to us but we drove them[.] today we are taking our ease & we need it for our men are worn down & beet out but are in good spirits for Lees Army is badly cut up & we have good news from Vicksburg & our troops are advancing on Richmond & if we do as well the next month as we have this it will soon end I hope it will.
   . . . I did think of sending home for a hat but I have one now[.] in the fight there was a reb behind a rock trying to shoot me but I was to quick for him my ball took him in the mouth & passed through his head so I took his hat. it is a hard saying but I cant help it[.] do not noise it about it. [He] was the only one that I know of hitting for sertain.
   Write as often as you can. . . . all of you I must stop & get dinner no more this time[.] my love & best wishes to you all & all inquiring friends.

Gene K

Payday

Lieutenant J. G. B. "Jack" Adams, had been severely wounded three times on July 2. Carried to a field hospital of the Third Corps, Adams was told he could not live twenty-four hours. On July 3 he was assured he would be removed to a hospital of the Second Corps. However, after an ambulance ride of only one mile, was "dumped" as he said, on the side of the road with several other men. The rest of the day he lay there, enemy shells falling nearby most of the afternoon. Finally, Adams and his wounded first sergeant were given a fast ambulance ride over a corn field "on the jump," as they recalled, and arrived at the corps hospital in terrible condition. A surgeon there told him, "It is a bad wound, John, a very bad wound."

One bullet had entered the groin and had not come out; the other had passed through his right hip. He remained there six days with no medical treatment. On July 10 he and a friend Duncan Sherwood, pooled their remaining $10 and rented a farmer and his wagon to take them to Littlestown where a train could be found. They remained in that town at a church for two days, where Adams' wounds became inflamed and he developed a high fever. Feeling he was soon to die, Adams was able to get himself placed on a train for Baltimore where he arrived at three o'clock on the morning of July 13 after a very tedious ride. He was taken to Newton University Hospital and for the *first time* his wounds were dressed. Lieutenant Adams explained:

. . . the surgeon placed a large syringe where the ball had entered and forced water through the opening; maggots, pieces of clothing and bone came out; then they probed for the ball which had entered the groin, found it had struck the bone and glanced downward, lodging in the leg where it yet remains. . . .

[Later] I did a foolish thing while in the hospital. . . . One day an officer . . . came in and said the paymaster was at the Custom House and if we could get there we would receive two month's pay. On the bed next to mine lay Lieut "Bob" Stewart of the 72nd Pennsylvania, wounded in the leg; neither of us had a dollar. . . . We talked it over . . . Bob was sure he could stand it . . . I was anxious to go, so we bribed the nurse, and the next morning, after the surgeon made his rounds, we took a carriage . . . for the Custom House. I fainted before we had gone a block, but kept on and was able to sign the roll which a clerk brought to the carriage and received the money. We returned to the hospital and I suffered from fever all day. . . . It was several days before I regained what I had lost by my foolishness.

The Last Hours of Captain Billings

Captain Charles W. Billings, 20th Maine Infantry, was wounded in the knee on July 2 while fighting on the south slope of Little Round Top. He was soon carried to an old barn on the Michael Fiscel farm which held the most serious hospital cases of the Fifth Army Corps. A delegate of the Christian Commission, Reverend Parvin told the rest of the story.

The brave fellow had some of his own men lying on the floor not far from him. He loved them with a father's love. As one after another died before his eyes, it worked so upon his mind that he became delirious, until it took four or five men to hold him. With great difficulty we got him away from his men into a room by himself, where he rallied and became a little better.

Once as I was passing [where he lay] the Surgeon came out; he told me the Captain must die. I entered and took him by the hand. His first words were –

'Chaplain, what did the Surgeon say?'

'Why, Captain, you are in a critical case.'

'I know that, Chaplain, but does he think I can live?'

'He thinks it hardly possible that you will.'

'Have you heard from my wife, Chaplain, since your message yesterday?'

'No; the telegraph lines are in the hands of the Government, but I hope she will be here.'

'. . . I would like to see my wife.'

'Well, Captain, if you have anything to say to her, . . . send the message by me.'

He asked me to give her his haversack, sword and some other little things, with a message. Dismissing then all earthly things from his mnd, he said to me –

'Don't stay any longer with me, Chaplain; go and help the boys. . . . '

Once afterwards he asked me to have his body embalmed and sent home. I promised to do so. He did not even refer to it again, but passed away in triumph.

It was in the morning at eleven o'clock that he died. [July 15] . . . Late that night, as I was busy writing letters from memoranda taken through the day, there was a knock at the door. In stepped a man inquiring for Captain Billings. . . .

'Who are you?' I asked.

'I am his brother, I have his wife with me! I have kept her up all the way with the hope that we would find the Captain in good condition. Where is he, sir?'

'You have not brought the Captain's wife out here to-night?'

(The Corps hospital was four miles from town.)

'No I left her in town until the morning.'

'That was well. The body of your brother was sent to the embalmers this afternoon.'

'Oh,' said he, 'I cannot tell her, I cannot trust myself to try to tell her, or even to see her again to-night;' –

The poor man broke down in his grief.

'I have brought her on all the way to Gettysburg for this, and now you must – you must tell her all.'

And so our duty was to see the bereaved wife, and deliver to her the messages and tokens of the dying love of her husband, and to speak the words of comfort in the name of the Lord.

Buttered Up

A nice recollection was given by relief agent John Patterson, who also worked for a while for the Christian Commission, and who had the opportunity to bring in some good country butter to a field hospital from one of the nearby Pennsylvania farms.

Quite a number of us had been busy aiding the Surgeons, who had attended to about two hundred cases of amputation during the day. . . . the [wounded] men were washed and dressed, [and] at supper they began bragging about our good butter.

'Let us see, boys,' said I, 'which of you can make the best wish for the old lady who made the butter.'

'An' shure,' replied an Irishman, 'may iv'ry hair of her hid be a wax candle to light her into glory,' – a kind of beautified Gorgon, one would say. Then came another Irish man's wish:

'May she be in hivin two wakes before the divil knows she's did.'

The third and last was from a son of the Emerald Isle likewise; it was addressed to myself;

'An' troth, sir, I hope God'll take a loikin' to yursilf!'

The Lock of Hair

A Massachusetts soldier was mortally wounded in the fighting at Gettysburg. When he died, his comrades tenderly buried him near one of the Union field hospitals. Soon afterwards the boy's mother wrote to Reverend Parvin, the Christian Commission relief agent who, as mentioned earlier was doing good work on that terrible field.

The mother begged the agent for "only one lock of his hair." Reverend Parvin said that a friend of the dead soldier dug down into the grave and severed a damp lock from the boy's mouldering head. It was soon sent on its mournful errand.

A Little Thing

Reverend George Bringhurst, another relief agent of the U.S. Christian Commission, liked to tell this story of his work in the field hospitals at Gettysburg.

One very dark night I met a soldier whose arms had both been shot away. He was getting to his tent, and I asked what I could do for him.

'Oh, nothing, Chaplain,' said he, cheerfully; 'unless you would tie my shoes for me. They have been bothering me a good deal.'

The Judge Presides

One of the most important tasks which had to be attended to after the battle was the burying or burning of the carcasses of several thousand dead horses and mules which had been left on the field. Much of this work was accomplished by the provost marshal's guard and a few unwounded Confederate prisoners who still remained in the area. The work was more than could be speedily accomplished by these few men, so another class of laborers was recruited.

These were some of the thousands of curious visitors who flocked to the field for one reason or another. The provost guard soon began to order anyone found taking relics from the battlefield to dig graves or hospital latrines for a span of twenty-four to forty-eight hours. One of these unfortunates was a Pennsylvania judge who was caught with a musket.

J. Howard Wert explained:

[The Judge] was a big man at home. His word was law. So when walking off with a fine specimen of firearms and told by a guard to drop it, he haughtily told the fellow in blue to mind his own business or he would report him to headquarters. . . .

That silly speech was his finish. Martial law respects no persons. It takes no more account of a judge than a hod carrier. So to burying horses he went. . . .

The day was a hot one. The work was new to the Judge. It was entirely out of his usual line. Soon his hands were woefully blistered. I am sorry to say that, although a Judge, he used profane language about the matter. . . .

The Judge was kept at work by spells for forty eight hours. [When the Judge] left Gettysburg. . . . I don't believe [he] ever hankered after visiting another battlefield.

The story was too good to keep and leaked out. It appeared in the Gettysburg *Star and Banner* of July 30th, 1863, no name being given. Then some of the Philadelphia papers got it and gave the details more fully, supplying also the name of the judicial laborer [who interred] battlefield horses. These papers were of opposite political faith to that of the Judge, and it was a sweet morsel to them.

Irish Jewels

Captain Nickerson, the survivor in this book's story, "Water, Water, Everywhere," had yet another craving which went unsatisfied for a long time.

Several weeks after the battle the hospitals became more and more organized, and the once famished and filthy wounded were now almost in the lap of luxury. Every imaginable type of delicacy poured in from generous and sympathetic civilians. Nickerson said that, "One corner [of my] tent was literally packed with all sorts of canned provisions, baskets of champagne, . . . wines, . . . (etc.)" But it wasn't enough.

And yet with the whimsical notions of a sick man, I had conceived the idea that there was nothing in the world I wanted or could eat except a roasted potato; and as it was said that there was not a potato to be had within miles of our camp, of course I wanted one more than ever. I had long since ceased asking for them, but when food was mentioned that simple vegetable was the only thing that suggested itself to my mind.

[A] clergyman friend was located [in a hospital nearby]. But he always came to see me at least once a day, and I had my tent flaps turned back so that I could watch for his coming. One very hot Sunday morning I caught sight of him coming considerably earlier than was his usual custom. His coat was thrown across his arm, and the perspiration was rolling down his face, but when he looked up and saw me watching his approach he swung a little bundle he had tied in his handkerchief, and exclaimed, with all the enthusiasm of a boy: 'I've got them, cap-

102

tain, I've got them!' Sure enough, he soon laid before me a dozen potatoes, two of which he immediately washed with his own hands and roasted in the ashes.

I saw Tiffany's collection of diamonds at the Centennial of 1876, and also the most notable display of jewels ever made by one person in this country, when the wife of a distinguished New York millionaire wore her gorgeous collection at a Presidential reception in the White House, not many years ago; and yet I have never seen any diamonds, rubies, sapphires, or pearls that were at all comparable with the exquisite beauty of that cluster of Irish potatoes, brought to me at Gettysburg, on Sunday morning, so many years ago, by the Rev. J. E. Adams, of New Sharon, Me. He had walked in the broiling sun over ten miles to gratify an invalid's whim.

To Your Health!

Our well-known narrator, Azor Nickerson, reminisces once again:

On the evening of the second day's battle, as I was about to take charge of my detachment for the skirmish line, an officer rode up and tapped me on the shoulder. I turned, and there was my old friend [Captain John P. Blinn] an assistant adjutant general [of Harrow's brigade]. We had little time for exchange of greetings. . . . Just then the adjutant announced that my companies were ready, my friend and I shook hands; he returned to his division, and I went down to the skirmish line.

One day, when the Reverend Adams was visiting me, he casually remarked upon the similarity of my case with that of another officer in the Second Division hospital, in whom he was also greatly interested, and he mentioned Blinn's name. I then found that my friend was also so badly wounded that it was not thought possible for him to recover. Mr. Adams said he was so anxious to live, at least until his widowed mother, who had been telegraphed for, came. I then sent a message to Blinn, that if I was alive at ten the next morning, I would join him in a glass of wine, at least, we could each take one at the same moment.

We continued this long-distance greeting for several mornings until one day, [July 18] just before the time for my glass with Blinn, a message came to my father; [who had been staying with Nickerson during his recuperation]. Instead of opening the bottle of wine for me as had been his custom, he came over by my bunk, laid his hand gently on my forehead, and looking sadly out across the green fields toward the hospital of the Second Division, he said: 'Poor Captain Blinn can't drink with you this morning; he is dead.'

The Captain's Gold

Dr. J. W. C. O'Neal, a Gettysburg physician, related the following, which he heard from a wounded Confederate colonel while visiting the U.S. General Hospital, one mile east of Gettysburg.

A Federal Captain had fallen at the 1st Battle of Bull Run. He was in a dying condition. Col. Herbert of the Md. Brigade, C. S. A. dismounted from his horse to place the expiring officer in an easier position with his head to rest on the moss covered root of a near tree. In the act his pocket book fell out. A Confederate soldier stooped to secure it, but the Col. said 'No, I'll take care of that.' At his leisure, an examination revealed the name of the dead officer to be a Capt. Brown of N.Y. – $57 in gold, and some important papers. Through the vicissitudes of Army life, when so many were suffering for food, and when gold would have answered a most merciful need and some of the command knew of the Col.'s charge of a respectable sum of gold, [however] nothing could move the Col. from his honorable and noble purpose.

At the Battle of Gettysburg, the Col. was severely wounded. And whilst lying at the Gen. Hospital – Camp Letterman, near G., he heard a lady in passing his tent, and learning that Confederates were in there, said I wonder if any of them know about my husband. She mentioned the name of Capt. Brown, which aroused the Col.'s attention. Satisfying himself as to the case, [he] replied, 'I may know something of your husband.' Her eyes glowed with hope. She had been hunting some word, etc. of her husband ever since the battle of Bull Run but so far in vain. The Col. produced the papers of the deceased he had in his possession and then counted down the $57 in gold, which he kept under trying difficulties until he should be able to hand it or send it with certainty, to the rightful owner. The feelings of the long distressed widow under such a generous gesture from a foe too, can better be imagined than described.

Lieutenant Colonel James R. Herbert was born in Woodstock, Maryland, in 1833. He enlisted as lieutenant of Company A, 1st Maryland Infantry, C. S. A., in early 1861, and rose to the rank of lieutenant colonel by January, 1863. He was wounded in the leg, arm, and abdomen at Gettysburg. Herbert died in Baltimore in 1884.

The Union officer was probably Captain David Brown, 79th New York Infantry, who was listed as "missing in action" on July 21, 1861 at Bull Run, Virginia. Officially, he was not listed as "killed" until after the war.

Rebel's Retreat

Anna M. Holstein, a Philadelphia volunteer nurse, recorded a humorous tale which occurred at the U.S. General Hospital on the York

Pike just east of Gettysburg. She was matron of this hospital, Camp Letterman, until its close in November, 1863.

> While the wounded were being brought in from different directions, a *rebel* was placed in a tent of *Union* men; one of the number protested against having him among them. As they seemed to pay no heed to his objections, ended [it] by saying that 'he enlisted to kill rebels, and certainly [if] they left him there, his crutches would be the death of [the Confederate] – he could use *them* if not the musket.' The attendants, finding the soldier was in earnest and the rebel in mortal fear of him, good humoredly took him among his own countrymen.

Back from the Dead

Nurse Holstein chronicled this interesting story with a somewhat happy ending.

> In another portion of the hospital was a man from Western Pennsylvania, whom his friends mourned as dead; whose funeral sermon had been preached, and his name on the rolls marked 'killed in battle.' His captain and comrades saw him fall in the midst of a desperate charge, and almost without a struggle life was gone – as they thought, and so reported.
>
> But it was not so; the bullet, in its course, went crashing through both eyes, though sparing life. A few hours later, when the wounded were gathered up; they found him . . . [and he was] taken with others to the hospital, [where] he lay for weeks unconscious, his brain affected from the inflammation which ensued. He could give no history of himself; but when hungry, would make it known by calling 'mother;' and talk to her constantly – first about his food, then of home concerns. I have heard him in these sad wanderings when he would ask: 'What do the girls say about me, now I have gone to the war? Does Jenny miss me?' and so on.
>
> At length his parents heard of him, and from the description thought it might be the son they mourned as dead. I was in his tent when his father came, and recognized in the blind, deranged man, his handsome, brave boy. Eventually his mind would be restored, but his sight never. In this state he took him home to the mother he talked of so much.

The Girls of Gettysburg

War time causes changes in social behavior. A good example of this is in how the civilian population may view enemy soldiers. In war, civilians usually put on a strong "front" for the benefit of the boys on the fighting lines. Later as time and the war drag on, and towns or territories are overrun by invading armies, these same non-combatants learn that they must adapt to stay healthy. This may mean doing a lot of things that your soldiers may not approve of, but it happens anyway. In fact due to the scarcity of young men, it was a common occurrence to see local women fraternizing with enemy soldiers. This situation developed even in Gettysburg, due to the large number of wounded Rebel prisoners left behind in the field hospitals near the town. Two examples are described below.

Major Henry K. Douglas, a wounded and captured Confederate who was recuperating at the Lutheran Theological Seminary near the town recalled:

"Nearby lived two young ladies who were great favorites in the Hospital because their generous hearts did not, apparently, distinguish the color of uniforms – loyal as they were – and on occasional nights, when Dr. Ward was conveniently absent or not visible, I would stroll with them to make visits in the town, . . . we generally landed at Duncan's and made an evening of it."

In a letter dated October 8, 1863, Captain H. L. Johnson, assistant adjutant general at "York District" headquarters located in Gettysburg wrote to Surgeon Henry Janes, commander of all hospitals in the area:

"Surgeon Janes, I am directed by Brig. Gen'l Ferry to call your attention to the fact that Rebel Prisoners both officers & men are allowed to visit Gettysburg upon passes issued by you. It is reported that Rebel officers have been seen in town as late as 11 o'clock P.M. in company with females.

"It is not deemed conducive to the best interests of the service to grant such permits . . .

Not Quite Dead

About six weeks after the Battle of Gettysburg, a wounded soldier recuperating in the town, read about himself in a Washington, D.C. newspaper. Here is his letter to the editor of that esteemed "rag."

Gettysburg, Sept. 1, 1863

Editor, *Star:*
I have just finished reading my obituary notice, published sometime since in the Washington "Daily Star," and though I feel highly complimented by the enumeration of my many virtues, etc. and the elegant style in which it is written, yet I am afraid it may have caused my friends great uneasiness.

I would therefore state that, to the best of my knowledge and belief, I am not dead; or at least, the facts in regard to my death have been very much exaggerated; and overstated, as I am now enjoying the hospitalities of kind people in Gettysburg to the fullest extent.

H. W. Walker

Getting Rich on Death: The Undertaking of Gettysburg

The environs of Gettysburg must have been a mortician's paradise from July 4 to November 20. On that date, when the last hospital closed and the dying ended, the services of these men were no longer required. However, until that time, the dead furnished a lucrative living to a small army of these opportunists.

The battle had caused the immediate death of over seven thousand men, and in the four-and-one-half months following, hundreds more died in the field hospitals. Many families wanted their fathers, sons and husbands buried at home, creating a boom in the embalming trade and the coffin business. A few eyewitnesses remembered these somber fellows and their melancholy wares. John C. Wills of the Globe Inn hotel, said:

> There were two Embalming rooms in town, one was in the room on York St. adjoining the Judge Wills building. The other was in the Brick School House on the Mummasburg road. At that time a number of our citizens made quite a good thing out of this gruesome business, of taking up the dead for those people and assisting them in preparing them for shipment to their home. Men who were engaged in this work bought whiskies in Large quantities, to prevent sickness in their work. . . . A number of them were . . . selling [the liquor] to soldiers at extortionate prices.

One man who made a sound living in the work described by Wills was John G. Frey. As an example, on November 17, 1863, he wrote the following to George Rider in Michigan explaining how he would send Rider's two dead sons home who had been mortally wounded in the battle.

> Dear Sir,
> I took those bodies today and found the boxes, by laying in the Ground so long all bursted so that I was compeled to have 2 new zinc coffins made and also Rough boxes which just cost me coffins, Boxes taken up and delivery at the depot $32.00 thirty-two Dollars, which would leave just $20.00 owing me which you will please send by my Express, for my trouble. I make no bill only what it cost me. . . .

Albertus McCreary, a young civilian, recalled the coffins:
"A man came to the town with patent coffins, and many a poor fellow took his last journey in one of them. The lid had a box in which ice was placed, thus making it possible to take bodies any distance."

Private Justus M. Silliman, 17th Connecticut Infantry, recovering from a wound at the U.S. General Hospital just east of town, wrote on August 2:

> . . . Since the battle Gettysburg has been an extensive coffin mart & embalmers harvest field. [T]he coffins were stacked on the streets blockading the side walks. [T]hese coffin speculators made an enormous profit but their harvest is now over, as the commander of this post has issued orders prohibiting the disinterring [of] any bodies during the months of August & Sept. . . .

Two other visitors commented on the large number of coffins. Chaplain

William C. Way, 24th Michigan Infantry, reported:

> It is saddening to stand near the office of the Express Company
> and see the coffined remains of scores and even hundreds,
> being sent to their former homes to be buried among friends.
> Many are dying, and it is almost impossible to get a coffin for
> their remains, so great is the demand for them.

Mrs. Henry May, a volunteer nurse, added;

> On the 11th of July 1863 I with much difficulty fought my way
> through Baltimore and secured permission from the Provo [sic]
> Marshall to proceed to Gettysburg, making the last few miles of the
> journey, from Hanover Junction in a box car loaded with empty
> coffins, upon which we were obliged to lie down and sleep.

So when visiting the Soldiers' National Cemetery at Gettysburg, one
should remember that he or she is viewing probably less than one-third of
the graves of *Union* men who were actually killed in, or died shortly after,
the battle, and of course, *none* of the Confederates.

Embalmer at work.

TO THE UNDERTAKER

OR FRIENDS WHO OPEN THIS COFFIN.

AFTER removing or laying back the lid of the Coffin, remove entirely the pads from the sides of the face, as they are intended merely to steady the head in travelling. If there be any discharge of liquid from the eyes, nose or mouth, which often occurs from the constant shaking of the cars, wipe it off gently with a soft piece of cotton cloth, slightly moistened with water.

This body was received by us for embalmment in a *Very Good* condition, the tissues being *Very Slightly discolored* The embalmment is consequently *Good* The natural expression is _____ preserved, on account of *the condition* in which it was received. The body will keep well for *any length of time*

After removing the coffin lid, leave it off for some time, and let the body have the air.

Drs. BROWN & ALEXANDER,
EMBALMERS,
WASHINGTON, D. C.

A Rebel Took His Place

The November 3, 1863 edition of the Adams *Sentinel* reported this interesting case of mistaken identity.

In the battle of Gettysburg there was engaged with the Union Forces a young man, whose parents reside in Birmingham, Allegheny county, Penna. It was announced that he was amoung the killed . . . and his friends proceeded to the battlefield to recover his remains. After some difficulty, they managed to recover what they were positive was his body, and brought it home and had it interred in the family burying ground. A few nights since, the house of the parents was visited by a young man from the army who aroused the household. On entering the house what was the surprise and astonishment of the parents to discover in their visitor their deeply mourned son, whose remains they fancied were resting quietly in the cemetery. It turned out that the body brought [home] . . . was that of a rebel, who wore in the battle a United States uniform and whose resemblance to the Union soldier was a very striking one.

PART VI

Post War

David Wills' Version

A postwar veterans' newspaper gave this report of where Abraham Lincoln's "Gettysburg Address" was actually written.

Lawyer [David] Wills, of Gettysburg, in whose house President Lincoln wrote the great speech that he delivered at the dedication of the Soldiers' National Cemetery in 1863, was in town this week, to attend to some business in the United States Circuit Court. 'All sorts of stories as to the circumstances attending the writing of this speech have been abroad,' he said. 'The truth in brief is this: Mr. Lincoln was a guest at my house. About 6 on the evening before the day of the dedication, he said that he had his speech to prepare. He got pens and paper and went up-stairs. He came down about 8:30. He asked where he could find Mr. [William H.] Seward. I replied that Mr. Seward was staying at Mr. [Robert G.] Harper's, who lived next door to me. He went in and found Mr. Seward. He carried a paper rolled up in his hand. I sat beside him next day, and heard him read the speech from that same paper. I have a lithographic copy. So you see the speech was not written while he was riding on a railroad car, or in any place other than my house.'

Brothers in "Arms"

Two brothers, Jack and Jasper Walker of Charlotte, North Carolina, fought at Gettysburg with the 13th North Carolina Infantry. Jasper, the younger, was wounded on July 1, as the fifth color bearer of his regiment to be shot. His leg was amputated; he was later captured by the enemy and sent to a Northern prison.

On the retreat from Gettysburg Brother Jack was also wounded and lost his left leg by amputation. He too was captured and ended up in another Federal military prison camp.

The brothers returned home after the war to become prosperous citizens, familiar to everyone in town as they stumped about on cork legs. On Jasper's wedding day, when he accidently fell and broke his artificial limb, he borrowed the leg of his gallant brother – which was a perfect fit.

This, as Confederate veterans were fond of telling youngsters, was the only case on record in which one man was married while standing on the leg of another.

The End of a Family

An article in the Gettysburg *Star and Sentinel* on May 29, 1888, reported:

Clayton Hoke of Cumberland Township, shows us an interesting relic found by his wife on the farm of Hon. Edward McPherson, formerly owned by John S. Crawford, Esq., deceased. It is a part of decayed wooden head-board which bears in neat letters the following inscription: 'Capt. J. M. Gaston. Capt. T. C. Clark & Son. 42d Miss. Vols. Killed July 1, 1863.' This farm was a vast rebel hospital.

In July, 1980, a letter was received by the historian at Gettysburg National Military Park. In it, the great-great-granddaughter of Captain Clark, Ms. Pam Lee of Carrollton, Mississippi, wrote that Captain Thomas Good Clark and *two* sons, Jonathan and A. Henry all of Company I of that regiment, were killed on July 1.

Truly, this was as terrible a tragedy as befell any family, north or south, during the four long years of our bloody Civil War.

A Withered Arm

On a visit to the Army Medical Museum* in the early 1870s, Mary C. Ames reported a curiosity she found in one of the exhibit cases there.

The first specimen which confronts you on entering is a withered human arm, with contracted hand and clinched fingers, mounted on wires in a glass case on the window ledge. The sharp bone protrudes where it was shot off near the shoulder joint; every muscle is defined; the skin looks like tanned leather. It is not pleasant to look at. A thrilling story has been printed about this arm. I am sorry it is not wholly true. The one I have to tell will not please you as well, for it is not nearly as exciting. We were told that the shock of the cannon-shot, which took off this arm, carried it up into a high tree, where, a year or two after, its owner, a Gettysburg hero, revisiting the battle-field, discovered his lost member lodged in the branches, brought it down and bore it hither as a trophy.

The soldier *did* find his arm (I am telling the true story); but he found it in a corn field. By what mark he knew it I am not informed, but he declared it to be his arm, and brought it to the Museum as a first-class 'sensational specimen.'

As unusual as this story seems it is more plausible than you may at first believe. Many limbs were literally "shot off" during this tremendous three-day battle. And many such appendages could be readily seen littering the fields and woods. A case in point was recalled by nurse Sophronia Bucklin who, after visiting the late battleground, wrote:

. . . evidences of the horrid carnage . . . lay on every hand in fearful sights.

. . . right above my head, at one place, so close that it touched me, hung a sleeve of faded army blue – a dead hand protruding from the worn and blackened cuff – I could not but feel a momentary shudder.

Boots, with a foot and leg putrifying within, lay beside the pathway, and ghastly heads too – over the exposed skulls of which insects crawled – while great worms bored through the rotting eyeballs.

*Now called the Armed Forces Medical Museum.

Georgia Gold

During the 1870s several of the former Confederate states made efforts to exhume the bodies of the Southern soldiers who were killed at Gettysburg. These remains were then transported to North Carolina, Georgia, Virginia, etc., where they were reinterred in local cemeteries. Also during this period, some families attempted to locate individual soldiers – sons or fathers or husbands – who had been slain during the great battle.

Of interest is the next story concerning Private Josiah H. Law, Company B, 4th Georgia Infantry, and Lieutenant Colonel David R. E. Winn of the same regiment. Both men were killed on July 1 and had been buried on the David Blocher farm just north of the town. R. B. Weaver, who made contact with the families of these men and with Blocher, finally succeeded in obtaining what was left of the corpses, and had them expressed to Savannah, Georgia. However, when the bodies arrived one family noticed that something was missing. Mr. Blocher had taken the gold dental plate out of the skull of Private Law and refused to return it. Weaver, in writing to Law's relatives in 1871, said:

> I had quite a time about the plate. I went out to B's several times and finally came [home] without the plate. . . . The next day I went out to see Oliver [Blocher] – met him and also saw the father. I resorted to everything possible to get the plate (except by money) but to no good effect. Just as I was going I said, 'Now what will bring that plate!' He said, 'You can write to them [the family], that if they would rather have the plate than a ten dollar bill why they can have it.' I asked if nothing short of that would bring the plate and he said No!

Weaver finally retrieved the gold teeth. Several weeks later he sent Blocher the money and the plate was reunited with its owner – the body of Private Law, C. S. A.

The Tale of a Ramrod

The following was found in an article printed in a Gettysburg newspaper in August of 1878.

> Last Sunday, as a party of the Grand Army of the Republic boys were visiting a portion of the battle-field, near the spot where the gallant Gen. [John F.] Reynolds fell, one of the boys said he remembered while he was in the hottest of the fight, and loading his rifle, his ramrod became fast in his gun so he could not extract it; so putting on a cap, he 'let sliver' at a rebel. Being close to him, he was certain the rod went through him. Just beyond the rebel stood a tree, which he thought he could find, if still standing. So the boys proposed to go with him and look. After searching a short time he discovered his tree, and the identical ramrod deeply embedded in its body. It is somewhat of a miraculous circumstance.

The Lost Grave

In the evening attack on July 2 which was made by Hoke's and Hays' Confederate brigades against the Union position on Cemetery Hill, Isaac E. Avery, the thirty-five-year-old colonel of the 6th North Carolina Infantry, was wounded. Although he had been wounded twice before in other battles this one was mortal, and he died the next day. His last message was written on a small bloodstained piece of paper. It read, "Tell father that I died with my face toward the enemy."

On the retreat from Gettysburg, Avery's body was taken along to be delivered to his family. When the army reached the Potomac River at Williamsport, Maryland, it was unable to cross immediately due to high water. While there, the colonel's remains were interred in an oak coffin under a pine tree in a small cemetery overlooking the river. W. C. Storrick disclosed this in 1931:

> Thirty years later, Judge A. C. Avery, of the Supreme Court of North Carolina, a resident of Morgantown, and Captain J. A. McPherson of Fayette, North Carolina, both veterans of the Confederacy came to Williamsport with the object of locating Colonel Avery's grave. Their search was fruitless.

Today, the site of this unfortunate officer's last resting place is still unknown.

Cooked Goose

On July 4, 1863, several members of a foraging party under Corporal John L. Smith, Company K, 118th Pennsylvania Infantry, who, following in the wake of the Confederate retreat, came to the D. Keefauver farm a couple of miles southwest of Gettysburg. While waiting for the remainder of the regiment, the men being hungry, beguiled Smith into paying seventy-five cents to Mrs. Keefauver for a "good-appearing" goose. Another seventy-five was added and Mrs. Keefauver agreed to cook said goose. What happened next was recollected by one of the infantrymen:

> In the light of after experience, the first investment was decidedly poor, but the sum paid to the worthy lady for the cooking was scarcely enough, for it took her *seven hours* to prepare that ancient feathered delicacy.
>
> Presently she brought it proudly forth, cooked, ready for the feast. The officers . . . [who had appeared at the opportune moment] as became their position as officers and brave men, first attacked it, but they were retired in great disorder. Then the men of the company were given a chance at the enemy, and it is recorded that they 'grew corns on their teeth' endeavoring to masticate the bird. It was defeat, black defeat.

In 1913, while attending the 50th Anniversary observance of the battle, several of these men gathered at the Keefauver farm to discuss the incident.

> There, on the green lawn they assembled and swapped yarns.
>
> Corp. John L. Smith gave the inside history of that famous goose episode. The corporal said that the farmer's son afterward

told him in strict confidence the family regretted exceedingly that they parted with the bird, as it had *been in the family for nineteen years!*

Others recalled how the obstinate feathered animal was finally taken into a nearby field by the defeated soldiers, and after being dismembered with an axe, was buried.

'Aye,' interrupted another of the regiment, 'and then the axe wasn't any further use, [so] we threw it away.'

The Youngest Veteran

On a cold Lincoln's birthday in February 1941, many, many miles west of Gettysburg, an old man died. His passing may have gone unnoticed, except the folks in Billings, Montana, considered him to be a celebrity of sorts.

The seventy-seven-year-old gentleman was Lewis Kenneth McClellan, and people thereabouts considered him to be a famous veteran; in fact at one time he was known as the "youngest veteran of the Battle of Gettysburg." McClellan's claim to fame happened this way:

He was the son of John Lewis McClellan and Georgia Wade McClellan who lived on Baltimore Street in Gettysburg. Little Lewis was born on June 26, 1863, the day Confederate troops first occupied the village and a few days prior to the famous battle.

It was in the McClellan house that baby Lewis spent his first few days of life. This would not have been an unusual situation, except that during his fifth, sixth, and seventh days he was surrounded by the terrible sounds of combat as battle raged over, around and even through the brick walls of his new environment.

Since his father was a Union soldier, and was many miles away during his birth and the days following, the care of Lewis was split between mother Georgia and an aunt, Mary Virginia "Jennie" Wade. Jennie Wade had made the dangerous decision to stay with sister McClellan to aid her in running the household. The knowledge that the house stood between the Federal and Confederate fighting lines did not seem to deter Jennie or Georgia. It should have, however, because on July 3 a bullet, possibly fired by a sharpshooter in the John Rupp tannery office on Baltimore Street, entered the small house where it struck and killed Mary Virginia Wade.

Infant Lewis knew none of this of course, until many years later. He grew up with his history, and in about 1906 moved to Montana. He had been a resident of Billings for sixteen years when he died. McClellan was survived by a wife, two sons, a sister and a brother, none of whom incidentally, resided within a thousand miles of Gettysburg.

A Tribute to Sergeant Nick Wilson

Nicholas George Wilson did not participate in the Battle of Gettysburg, and in fact, was over a hundred miles away at the time it was being fought.

However, ironically, Wilson, who had no direct connection with the great event, spent thirty years of his life preserving, monumenting and maintaining the battlefield for its veterans and future generations.

Nicholas or "Nick" Wilson was born in 1832 in Wilsonville (now Bendersville), Pennsylvania as the great-grandson of one of the first settlers of that beautiful area of Adams County. His early occupations included farming, but he predominantly worked as a teamster and blacksmith. Wilson married twice, once in 1852 and again in 1857, after the death of his first wife. He and his wives, Willimina Eyster and Elenora Walter, had two children, both daughters.

In 1861, Wilson joined a state militia unit and remained with this company until July 2, 1862. He was then mustered as the first sergeant of Company G, 138th Pennsylvania Infantry, a position he held until the end of the war. Sergeant Wilson participated in several campaigns and more than ten battles. In July of 1864 he was severely wounded at the Battle of Monocacy. This wound effectively brought his campaigning to an end.

Discharged in May, 1865, Nick Wilson returned to his former occupation of teaming. Three years later, although crippled, he built his first home, a brick house on Liberty (Rampike) Hill in Bendersville, using the foundation of a much earlier structure that he had inherited from his grandfather in 1859.

On the first of July, 1873, Wilson was appointed Superintendent of the Soldiers' National Cemetery in Gettysburg, a post he held for almost fifteen years. In late 1887 he accepted the position of superintendent of grounds for the Gettysburg Battlefield Memorial Association, where he remained employed until 1895 when the grounds were transferred to the United States government. During these years, Wilson planned and directed the construction of nearly all of the avenues on the Union lines of battle, and participated in like manner in the erection of over 350 monuments on the battlefield. N. G. Wilson was also a member of Corporal Skelly Post No. 9, Department of Pennsylvania, Grand Army of the Republic from 1873 until his death. He served as commander and quartermaster during that time.

Until his death in October, 1907, Nicholas Wilson led a busy life. He became a member of the Gettysburg Town Council; was elected to the Gettysburg School Board where he served as president for three years, became a representative to the Pennsylvania Legislature, also auditor of the Pennsylvania National Guard, and was a delegate to National and Department Encampments of the G.A.R. each year from 1873 – 1904.

His obituary summed up his character by saying:

"[Sergeant Wilson] was a whole-souled fellow and popular with everyone who knew him. . . . He was a man of much native ability, thoroughly doing all work intrusted to him and the development of this town and battlefield owe much to him. Personally he was most companionable, possessing those qualities of heart and mind that made those who knew him best admire and highly esteem him. . . ."

Today the house of this remarkable "Gettysburg preservationist" can still be seen in Bendersville, where his unassuming gravestone in the Lutheran cemetery nearby belies the "simple greatness" that truly rests beneath.

Sergeant Wilson's house in Bendersville.

N. G. Wilson about 1880.

We clashed together like waves on rocks,
We fought 'till the ground was red.
We met in the shuddering battle shocks,
Where none but the freed soul fled.

But now side by side in the nations life,
And shoulder to shoulder are we,
And we know by the grip of our hands in strife,
What the strength of our love may be.

William Averell

THE END

THE SOURCES

PART I

1. SIMON THE MULE
   Confederate Veteran. Vol. 5, 1897.
2. MUD MARCH
   Confederate Veteran. Vol. 5, 1897.
3. ALL "RAILED" UP
   Dickert, D. Augustus. *History of Kershaw's Brigade*. Dayton, OH: Morningside Press, 1973.
4. TRADEOFF
   McCurdy, Charles M. *Gettysburg: A Memoir*. Pittsburgh, PA: Reed & Witting Co., 1929.
5. FOOTSORE
   Pennsylvania at Gettysburg. Harrisburg, PA: Wm. Stanley Ray, State Printer, 1904.
6. ANOTHER KNAPSACK
   Confederate Veteran. Vol. 24, 1916.
   Fremantle, James A. *The Fremantle Diary*. Ed. Walter Lord. Boston, MA: Little, Brown & Co., 1954.
7. CAPTURED CIVILIANS
   History of Cumberland and Adams Counties, Penna. Chicago, IL: Warner, Beers, & Co., 1866.
   Unpublished diary of John B. Linn in Gettysburg National Military Park Library.
8. IN COLD BLOOD
   Nye, W. S. *Here Come The Rebels*. Baton Rouge, LA: Louisiana State University Press, 1965.
9. THE FIGHT AT THE WITMER FARM
   Richards, H. M. M. *Pennsylvania Emergency Men at Gettysburg: A Touch of Bushwhacking*. Reading, PA: private printing, 1895.
10. A MYSTERIOUS VISITOR
    Nye, W. S. *Here Come The Rebels*. Baton Rouge, LA: Louisiana State University Press, 1965.
11. A TERRIBLE MISTAKE
    "Encounter at Hanover: Prelude to Gettysburg," Hanover Chamber of Commerce, 1963.
12. TANNED
    New York at Gettysburg, Vol. III. Albany, NY: 1900.
13. A PERFECT FIT
    Land We Love. Monthly publication. Charlotte, NC: 1867.
14. "PIG OUT"
    Confederate Veteran. March, 1906.
15. PLENTY OF PLUNDER
    J. B. Polley, *Hood's Texas Brigade*. Press of Morningside Bookshop Dayton, OH: 1976.
16. ADAMS COUNTY'S LOSS
    Gettysburg Star & Sentinel, October, 1868, and files at Gettysburg National Military Park Library.
17. SPIES
    King, Sarah Barrett, "Battle Days in 1863," *Gettysburg Compiler*, July 4, 1906.
    Wills, John, interview published in *Gettysburg Compiler*, July 21, 1910.
    Myers, Elizabeth S., "How a Gettysburg School-teacher Spent Her Vacation in 1863," San Francisco *Sunday Call*, August 16, 1903.
    Other notes in author's research files.

PART II

18. THE FIGHTING BLACKS
    New York Herald, July 24, 1863.
19. THE DARING CAVALRYMAN
    Hard, Dr. Abner. *History of the Eighth Cavalry Regiment Illinois Volunteers During the Great Rebellion*. Aurora, IL: 1868.
20. SISTERS AND BROTHERS
    Daughters of Charity: Mother Regina and Mother Ann Simeon. Emmitsburg, MD: St. Joseph's, 1939.
    Fuller, C. A. *Personal Recollections of the War of 1861*. Sherburne, NY: News Job Printing House, 1905.
21. THE CHOICE
    News article in *Arbor State*, Wymore, NE, May 30, 1944 issue.
22. NAUGHTY JACK
    Cook, Captain J. D. S., "Personal Reminiscences of Gettysburg," *War Talks in Kansas*, (MOLLUS), 1903.

23. A PERFECT SHOT
    Cook, John H. *Reminiscences & Letters of George Arrowsmith of New Jersey.* Red Bank, NJ: 1893.
    A New Canaan Private in the Civil War, Letters of Justis M. Silliman. New Canaan Historical Society: 1984.
    Hoke, Jacob. *The Great Invasion of 1863.* Dayton, OH: W. J. S. Huey Publications, 1887.
24. JOHN SNYDER'S RUN
    Kiefer, Wm. R. *History of the 153rd Regiment PA Volunteers and Infantry.* Easton, PA: Chemical Publishing Co., 1909.
25. FACE DOWN
    Land We Love. Monthly Publication. Charlotte, NC: 1867.
26. A FIGHT UNFOUGHT
    Pfanz, H. W. *Gettysburg: The Second Day.* Chapel Hill, NC: University of North Carolina Press, 1987.
27. CAPTAIN IRSCH'S LAST STAND
    Beyer, W. F., and Keydel, O. F., eds. *Deeds of Valor.* Detroit, MI: 1906.
28. GENERAL LEE'S CRITICS
    Various references in author's research files.
29. ALIVE AND KICKING
    "Memoirs of the 2nd Maryland Battalion, C.S.A." *The Telegram,* Baltimore, MD: 1870s, in Gettysburg National Military Park Library.
30. THE IRISH THIEF
    Letter to Mrs. S. M. Stewart of Gettysburg from Richard Laracy, in Gettysburg National Military Park Library.

PART III

31. OLD GINGER FINGERS
    Gettysburg Compiler, December 27, 1898.
32. DRESSED TO KILL
    "Back in Rebellion Days," *Gettysburg Star and Sentinel,* August 28, 1907.
33. A DIRTY TRICK
    Unpublished diary of John B. Linn in Gettysburg National Military Park Library.
34. SHORT SWORD
    Livermore, Thomas L. *Days and Events 1860 – 1866.* Boston, MA & New York, NY: Houghton Mifflin Co., 1920.
35. MARKED FOR DEATH
    Wert, J. Howard, "In the Hospitals of Gettysburg," Harrisburg *Telegraph,* 1907.
36. A GOOD TIME FOR MISCHIEF
    McCreary, Albertus, *McClure's Magazine,* Vol. 33,
    July, 1909.
37. LET'S BUY 'EM
    The Grand Army Scout and Soldier's Mail, Vol. 5.
38. HE *FELT* THE FIRING
    McCreary, Albertus, "Gettysburg: A Boy's Experience of the Battle," *McClure's Magazine,* Vol. 33, 1909.
39. RIGBY'S REPAIRS
    Letter of Lieutenant Augustine N. Parsons, written from Summit, Texas, (Tyler County), June 2, 1889.
40. FOURTEEN DAYS
    Confederate Veteran. Vol. 19, 1911.
41. PITZER'S TREASURE
    McCurdy, Charles M. *Gettysburg: A Memoir.* Pittsburgh, PA: Reed & Witting Co., 1929.
    Unpublished diary of John B. Linn in Gettysburg National Military Park Library.
    Article in *Gettysburg Compiler,* August 19, 1884.
42. "RABBIT FIRE"
    Smith, John L. *History of the Corn Exchange Regiment.* Philadelphia, PA: 1888.
43. PENNSYLVANIA BISCUITS
    Polley, J. B. *Hood's Texas Brigade.* New York, NY: Neale Publishing Co., 1910.
44. NELSON'S FOLLY
    Oates, Wm. C. *The War Between the Union and the Confederacy.* Dayton, OH: Morningside Press, reprint 1974.
45. QUITE A TRIP
    Chase, Captain Dudley H. "Gettysburg," *Indiana War Papers* (MOLLUS, Indiana).

46. BRAVERY UNSURPASSED
   "The Fifth Corps at Gettysburg," *National Tribune,* July, 1915.
47. A TRICK OF THE MIND
   New York at Gettysburg, Vol. III. Albany, NY: 1900.
48. YANKEE "PONE"
   Manuscript, "War Story of George C. Pile," in Tennessee State Library and Archives.
49. CALIFORNIA CAKE
   National Tribune, March 23, 1911.
50. RETREAD!
   Morhous, Sergeant Henry C. *Reminiscences of the 123rd New York State Volunteers.* Greenwich, NY: 1879.
51. "PRAYING JOE" RICHARDSON
   Diary/Memoir of Sergeant James A. Wright at the Minnesota Historical Society.
52. HE IS THERE
   Kepler, Wm. *History of the Fourth Regiment Ohio Volunteer Infantry.* Cleveland, OH: Leader Printing Co., 1886.
53. HOG'S HEAVEN
   Smith, John L. *History of the Corn Exchange Regiment.* Philadelphia, PA: 1888.

PART IV

54. THE ENTERPRISING IRISHMAN
   Grand Army Review, Vol. I, #5.
55. FISHER'S LUCK
   Military and family records of Rolandes E. Fisher.
   Personal documents and artifacts in author's possession.
56. FIREWORKS!
   Smith, Donald L. *The Twenty-Fourth Michigan of the Iron Brigade.* Harrisburg, PA: The Stackpole Co., 1962.
57. ALMOST DRAFTED
   McCreary, Albertus, *McClure's Magazine,* Vol. 33, July, 1909.
58. THE MILLION DOLLAR WOUNDS
   Simpson, Wm. T., "The Drummer Boys of Gettysburg," Philadelphia *North American,* June, 1913.
59. CAPTAIN TOURISON'S LOSS
   Simpson, Wm. T., "The Drummer Boys of Gettysburg," Philadelphia *North American,* June, 1913.
60. SERGEANT HITCHCOCK'S GIFT
   General Alexander Hays at the Battle of Gettysburg. Pittsburgh, PA: privately printed, 1913.
61. TRUCE
   Galwey, Thomas F., "An Episode of the Battle of Gettysburg," *Catholic World,* July, 1881.
   Galwey, Thomas F. *The Valiant Hours.* Harrisburg, PA: 1961.
62. THE FLYING SURGEON
   Livermore, Thomas L. *Days and Events 1860 - 1866.* Boston, MA and New York, NY: Houghton Mifflin Co., 1920.
63. VOLUNTEER OR ELSE!
   Adams, Captain John G. B. *Reminiscences of the Nineteenth Massachusetts Regiment.* Boston, MA: Wright & Potter Printing Co., 1899.
64. SURGEON TAYLOR'S DELICATE WOUND
   Taylor, Dr. Wm. H., "Some Experiences of a Confederate Assistant Surgeon," *Transactions of the College of Physicians of Philadelphia,* Vol. 28, 1906.
65. SHELLFIRE
   Hanna, T. L., "A Day at Gettysburg," *National Tribune,* May, 1900.
66. THE COWARDLY COLOR BEARER
   Small, Abner R. *The Road to Richmond.* Berkeley, CA: University of California Press, 1939.
67. THE DYING VIRGINIAN
   Small, Abner R. *The Road to Richmond.* Berkeley, CA: University of California Press, 1939.
68. LITTLE BROTHER
   Wert, J. Howard. *A Complete Hand-book of the Monuments and Indications and Guide to the Positions on the Gettysburg Battlefield.* Harrisburg, PA: 1886.
69. THE FIGHTING SURGEON
   "Charge of Black's Cavalry Regiment at Gettysburg," *Confederate Veteran,* Vol. 16, 1888.
70. A CHINAMAN IN THE RANKS
   The Adams Sentinel, October 20, 1863.

71. GENERAL MEADE'S ADVICE
Storrs, John W. *The Twentieth Connecticut, A Regimental History.* Ansonia, CT: 1886.

72. TIPSY TIPPIN
Diary of Lewis Schaeffer in the library of the University of West Virginia.

73. THE DEADLY WINDMILL
Muffy, J. W., ed. *The Story of Our Regiment, 148th Pennsylvania Volunteers.* Des Moines, IA: 1904.

74. MOONLIT APPARITION
Carter, R. G. *Reminiscences of the Campaign and Battle of Gettysburg.* (MOLLUS, Maine), Vol. 3.

75. DISILLUSIONMENT AND DESERTION IN THE CONFEDERATE ARMY
Various references in author's research files.

PART V

76. THE OVERZEALOUS MR. PIERCE
Alleman, Matilda J. Pierce. *At Gettysburg: What a Girl Saw and Heard of the Battle.* New York, NY: W. L. Bortland, 1889.

77. CUT DOWN TO SIZE
Rittenhouse, Benjamin F. *The Battle of Gettysburg as Seen from Little Round Top.* (MOLLUS, District of Columbia), Vol. 3, 1887.

78. JUGS
Croll, Jennie S., "Days of Dread – A Woman's Story of Her Life on a Battlefield," Philadelphia *Weekly Press,* November, 1887.

79. GENERAL LEE'S PET
Davis, Burke. *Our Incredible Civil War.* New York, NY: Ballantine Books, 1960.

80. THE COLOR OF DEATH
Bloodgood, Reverend J. D., Ph.D. *Personal Reminiscences of the War.* New York, NY: Hunt & Eaton, 1898.

81. THE SHORT CUT
Article in Philadelphia *Weekly Press,* November, 1887.

82. A GOOD JOB
Tobie, Edward P. *History of the 1st Maine Cavalry.* Boston, MA: Press of Emery & Hughes, 1887.

83. TOUGHER THAN NECESSARY
Clark, Walter, ed. *Histories of the Several Regiments and Battalions from North Carolina . . . 1861-1865.* Goldsboro, NC: Nash Brothers, 1901.

84. GENERAL MEADE'S OTHER HEADQUARTERS
Files in the Gettysburg National Military Park Library.

85. WESTERN PLUCK
Wert, J. Howard, "In the Hospitals of Gettysburg," Harrisburg *Telegraph,* 1907.

86. FREE AT LAST
Jones, H. G. *To The Christian Soldiers and Sailors of the Union.* Philadelphia, PA: Lippincott's Press, 1868.

87. ONE FOOT IN THE GRAVE
Wert, J. Howard, *A Complete Hand-book of the Monuments and Indications and Guide to the Positions on the Gettysburg Battlefield,* Harrisburg, PA: 1886.

88. WATER, WATER, EVERYWHERE . . .
Nickerson, Azor H., "Personal Recall of Two Visits to Gettysburg," *Scribner's Magazine,* New York, 1893.

89. ALTERCATION AT MRS. WADE'S
Information courtesy of Edmund J. Raus, author of *A Generation on the March: The Union Army at Gettysburg*

90. MRS. HANNESS'S LONG SEARCH
Wert, J. Howard, "In the Hospitals at Gettysburg," Harrisburg *Telegraph,* 1907.

91. NOT OUT OF RANGE
Johnson, Clifton, *Battleground Adventures.* Boston, MA and New York, NY: Houghton Mifflin Co., 1915.

92. THE AWFUL NOISE OF BATTLE
Various references in author's research files.

93. PHOTOGRAPH OF A DEAD MAN
Conversation with Edward Guy.

94. PAPA'S BOY
Livermore, Thomas L. *Days and Events 1860 - 1866.* Boston, MA and New York, NY: Houghton Mifflin Co., 1920.

95. THE SPRING FORGE SCAVENGERS
Wert, J. Howard, "In the Hospitals at Gettysburg," Harrisburg *Telegraph,* 1907.

96. FEARFUL EXPECTATIONS
Foster, J. Y., "Four Days at Gettysburg," *Harper's Magazine,* February, 1864.

97. LYDIA SMITH – HEROINE
Wert, J. Howard, "In the Hospitals at Gettysburg," Harrisburg *Telegraph,* 1907.

98. THE SAGA OF "BIG TOM" NORWOOD
The Historian, Vol. 25, February, 1963.
Letter from Thomas L. Norwood at the University of North Carolina.

99. BONES
Notes in the Gettysburg National Military Park Library.

100. A "DEAR JOHN" LETTER
The Patriot Daughters of Lancaster. *Hospital Scenes after the Battle of Gettysburg.* Philadelphia, PA: 1864.

101. THE PRODIGAL COW
McCreary, Albertus, "Gettysburg: A Boy's Experience of the Battle," *McClure's Magazine,* Vol. 33, 1909.

102. THE LITTLE SOLDIER
Souder, Mrs. Edmund A. *Leaves from the Battle-field of Gettysburg.* Philadelphia, PA: Caxton Press, 1864.

103. DOOLEY'S STORY
Durkin, Joseph T., ed. *John Dooley, Confederate Soldier His War Journal.* Notre Dame, IN: University of Notre Dame Press, 1963.

104. HEADS UP
McKim, Randolph H. *A Soldier's Recollections.* New York, NY: 1910.

105. TO EACH HIS OWN
Elher, Mrs. C. A. *Hospital Scenes after the Battle of Gettysburg.* Philadelphia, PA: 1864.

106. THE WILD TEXAN
Article by Colonel R. M. Powell, Philadelphia *Weekly Press:* December, 1884.

107. DEADSHOT
Original letter in the possession of Glen Hayes, Pleasantville, NY.

108. PAYDAY
Adams, Captain John G. B. *Reminiscences of the Nineteenth Massachusetts Regiment.* Boston, MA: Wright & Potter Printing Co., 1899.

109. THE LAST HOURS OF CAPTAIN BILLINGS
Jones, H. G. *To the Christian Soldiers and Sailors of the Union.* Philadelphia, PA: Lippincott's Press, 1868.

110. BUTTERED UP
Jones, H. G. *To the Christian Soldiers and Sailors of the Union.* Philadelphia, PA: Lippincott's Press, 1868.

111. THE LOCK OF HAIR
Jones, H. G. *To the Christian Soldiers and Sailors of the Union.* Philadelphia, PA: Lippincott's Press, 1868.

112. A LITTLE THING
Jones, H. G. *To the Christian Soldiers and Sailors of the Union.* Philadelphia, PA: Lippincott's Press, 1868.

113. THE JUDGE PRESIDES
Wert, J. Howard, "In the Hospitals of Gettysburg," Harrisburg *Telegraph,* 1907.

114. IRISH JEWELS
Nickerson, Azor H., "Personal Recall of Two Visits to Gettysburg," *Scribner's Magazine,* New York, 1893.

115. TO YOUR HEALTH!
Nickerson, Azor H., "Personal Recall of Two Visits to Gettysburg," *Scribner's Magazine,* New York, 1893.

116. THE CAPTAIN'S GOLD
Unpublished physician's handbook of Dr. J. W. C. O'Neal, 1863, in Gettysburg National Military Park Library.

117. REBEL'S RETREAT
Holstein, Mrs. A. M. *Three Years in Field Hospitals of the Army of the Potomac.* Philadelphia, PA: 1867.

118. BACK FROM THE DEAD
Holstein, Mrs. A. M. *Three Years in Field Hospitals of the Army of the Potomac.* Philadelphia, PA: 1867.

119. THE GIRLS OF GETTYSBURG
Letter in author's files.

Douglass, Henry K. *I Rode With Stonewall*. Chapel Hill, NC: University of North Carolina Press 1940.

120. NOT QUITE DEAD
Wert J. Howard, "In the Hospitals of Gettysburg," Harrisburg *Telegraph,* 1907.

121. GETTING RICH ON DEATH: THE UNDERTAKING OF GETTYSBURG
Various references in author's research files.

122. A REBEL TOOK HIS PLACE
The Adams Sentinel, November 3, 1863.

PART VI

123. DAVID WILLS' VERSION
The Grand Army Sentinel, Vol. II, #22.

124. BROTHERS IN "ARMS"
Davis, Burke. *Our Incredible Civil War.* New York, NY: Ballantine Books, 1960.

125. THE END OF A FAMILY
Gettysburg Star and Sentinel, May 29, 1888.
Letter from Pam Lee, July 9, 1980 to Kathleen Georg Harrison, historian at Gettysburg National Military Park.

126. A WITHERED ARM
Ames, Mary C. *Ten Years in Washington.* Hartford, CT: A. D. Worthington & Co., 1873.
Bucklin, Sophronia E. *In Hospital and Camp.* Philadelphia, PA: John E. Potter & Co., 1869.

127. GEORGIA GOLD
Letter from R. B. Weaver to Mrs. R. L. Campbell, October 9, 1871, in Gettysburg National Military Park Library.

128. THE TALE OF A RAMROD
Gettysburg Compiler, August 2, 1878.

129. THE LOST GRAVE
Storrick, W. C. *The Battle of Gettysburg.* Harrisburg, PA: 1931.

130. COOKED GOOSE
Blake, W. H. *Hand Grips.* Private printing: 1913.

131. THE YOUNGEST VETERAN
The Gettysburg Times, February 13, 1941.

132. A TRIBUTE TO SERGEANT NICK WILSON
Gettysburg Compiler, December 11, 1907.
Newspaper clippings file at Gettysburg National Military Park Library.
Other notes in author's collection.

Other titles available from Thomas Publications:

Ready . . . Aim . . . Fire!
Small Arms Ammunition in the Battle of Gettysburg.
ISBN-0-939631-00-8

Small Arms 1856
Reports of Experiments with Small Arms for the Military Service, by
Officers of the Ordnance Department, U.S. Army. Washington: 1856
The story of the development of the U.S. Model of 1855 small arms and
ammunition.
ISBN-0-939631-01-6

Confederate Field Manual with photographic supplement
The Field Manual for the Use of the Officers on Ordnance Duty.
Richmond: 1862
Confederate ordnance material as it really was.
ISBN-0-939631-02-4

CANNONS
An Introduction to Civil War Artillery.
ISBN-0-939631-03-2

Parrott Guns
Ranges of Parrott Guns and Notes for Practice, by R.P. Parrott: 1862

Siege Artillery in the Campaigns against Richmond with Notes on the 15-
inch Gun, by Henry L. Abbott: 1868
ISBN-0-939631-04-0

Civil War Commanders
Concise biographies of 111 Union and Confederate commanders with
photographs.
ISBN-0-939631-05-9

The Gettysburg Battlefield Tour Book, by Michael R. McGough
The up-to-date guide to a 17-stop tour of the Gettysburg National Military
Park and Cemetery.
ISBN-0-939631-06-7

The Siege and Reduction of Fort Pulaski, by Brig. Gen. Q.A. Gillmore: 1862
The official report of the capture of Fort Pulaski, Georgia, made by the chief
engineer.
ISBN-0-939631-07-5

Soldiers' National Cemetery – Gettysburg: 1865
A collection of the documents concerning the establishment of the Gettys-
burg National Cemetery, including a list of Union burials.
ISBN-0-939631-08-3

A Vast Sea Of Misery

A History and Guide to the Union and Confederate Field Hospitals at Gettysburg, July 1–November 20, 1863

GREGORY A. COCO

Nearly twenty-six thousand men were wounded in the three-day battle of Gettysburg. It did not matter if the soldier was Union or Confederate, officer or enlisted man, for the bullets, shell fragments, bayonets, and swords made no class or sectional distinction. Of the injured combatants, almost 21,000 were left behind by the two armies, in and around the small village of 2,400 civilians. These maimed and suffering warriors lay in churches, public buildings, private homes, farmhouses, barns and out-buildings, and thousands, unable to move, remained in the open, subject to the uncertain whims of the July elements. All of these men were certainly trapped in the bloody jaws of death. The battle to save the wounded was as terrible as the battle which placed them in such a perilous position. As one surgeon unhappily recalled:

> . . . no written nor expressed language could ever picture the field of Gettysburg! Blood! blood! and tattered flesh! shattered bones and mangled forms almost without the semblance of human beings! faces torn and bruised and lacerated until wife or mother could hardly have recognized one of them! groans and cries! screams and curses! moans and grinding teeth! I . . . live over again those weeks of sick work, when the cut of the knife and the rasp of the saw seem to be grating upon my own overtaxed nerves. Oh, the horror! The misery! The terror of a battle! Gallant men . . . shattered into shapeless, breathing masses of broken bones and burned and torn flesh!

This book will take you into 160 of those frightful places called field hospitals. And after the journey you will never again feel quite the same about *GETTYSBURG*.

ISBN-0-939631-09-1

Gregory Ashton Coco was born in 1946 and grew up in Louisiana, where at the University of Southwestern Louisiana he received a Bachelor of Arts degree in history in 1972. From 1967 through 1969 Coco served in the U.S. Army, including a tour in Vietnam, where as a P.O.W. interrogator and infantryman he was twice wounded. In civilian life he has worked as a state trooper and city policeman; also as a battlefield guide, park ranger, historian, and maintenance worker/gardner at the Gettysburg National Military Park.

In 1981, Coco published his first book, *Through Blood and Fire: The Civil War Letters of Charles J. Mills.* He is also the author of *A Vast Sea of Misery: A History and Guide to the Union and Confederate Field Hospitals at Gettysburg,* as well as Volumes I and II of *On The Bloodstained Field;* in addition to various newspaper and magazine articles.

At the present time Coco is working on an account of the Confederate burials at Gettysburg, and is editing two soldiers' diaries and recollections for publication. He also frequently gives lectures and tours on a variety of topics dealing with the Civil War and especially the Campaign and Battle of Gettysburg.

The reader may contact the author through Thomas Publications, P.O. Box 3031, Gettysburg, PA 17325.

John S. Heiser was born and raised in Raleigh, North Carolina, an area rich in history. He has had an interest in the Civil War since the age of six, and continuing this interest, John received his degree in American History from Western Carolina University. An employee for the National Park Service since 1978, he has also contributed illustrations and maps for other works on the subject, including the three volumes of *The Vicksburg Campaign,* by Edwin Bearss. John recently married Carmen Johnson and is living in the Gettysburg area.

Bob Prosperi was born in Scotland County, North Carolina, and has lived most of the last thirty years on or near the Gettysburg battlefield. A U.S. Army veteran, he holds a BA in history from Indiana University of Pennsylvania. Since 1976 Bob has worked at the Gettysburg National Military Park, first as a park ranger and has been a park historian since 1985.

" Pards "